Mother Hen Flew the Coop

Mother Hen Flew the Coop

The Book For Moms Who Feel Like Crap

Melissa Harding

ISBN: 0692736670
ISBN 13: 9780692736678

Cover design by Jenny Randle
www.JennyRandle.com

For Selah, Gavin and Emery.
You have unraveled my small view of God.
Thank you, sweet ones.

Table of Contents

Mother Hen Flew the Coop

I must confess something to you: I used to be a really great mom. In fact, I used to be the best mom.

I always had a soft answer for my children. I welcomed them home from school with cookies fresh out of the oven. We played games, and I loved every second of it. I loved sitting on the floor, playing with Barbies, and I never snuck glances at my phone while playing with Legos. I made all of our meals from scratch. We made elaborate crafts with glue, glitter and paint, and I never stressed over the mess. I never worried. Or cried. Or yelled. We danced in the rain and made mud pies on the driveway. My children never fought. Or whined. Or complained. I laughed when they did something wrong, and I never counted the minutes until bedtime. Yes, I was a pretty darn good mama.

I was also 8 years old playing house.

All I ever wanted to be was a mom. While some girls dream of making it to the Olympics, making a name in the corporate world or pouring knowledge into the minds of young students, I dreamed of carrying babies close to my chest and running through fields of wildflowers with a flock of little chicks in tow.

I was going to be the best mom that ever walked this earth.

Now that my 8-year-old dreams have culminated in a very raw, life-sucking reality, I've come to realize one very important thing: I could be a good mom — if it weren't for my children.

I mean, really. I wouldn't need to raise my voice if it weren't for them, right? I wouldn't be stressed out if it weren't for them. I would sleep through the night if it weren't for them instead of lying awake thinking about every tiny thing that could possibly ever happen to them.

I didn't worry about pianos falling on tiny limbs before I became a mom.

I didn't worry about the mind-draining effects of technology before I became a mom.

I would have far less wrinkles, heartburn, panic attacks, stretch marks and fat rolls if it weren't for them.

All I ever wanted to be was a mom, and some days, all I want to be is anything *other than* a mom. When the Cheerios spill, the kids fight and my best is something short of a raging lunatic, I look back on the mom I thought I would be. I look for the mom who wanted to gather her chicks close and never let them go.

In her place, I see a mom who flew the coop and headed straight to crazy town.

Yes, I could be a good mom if that flock of little chicks didn't get in the way. And yet, if it weren't for them, I wouldn't know the depths and riches of God's grace. I wouldn't know how to fall utterly and totally help-less at the feet of Jesus when my anger gets the best of me. I wouldn't have learned how to lean against the heart of Jesus, learning to rest, to give up my failures as I hear the steady beat of His love for me. I wouldn't know the peace that comes from giving up my dreams as I'm overwhelmed with the heart-gripping reality that God's dreams for myself and my children exceed my greatest expectations.

I could be a good mom if it weren't for my kids. But I don't want to be a good mom anymore; I want to be a mom who knows her worth in Jesus alone. I want to be a mom who lays down her perceptions of perfect and allows her children to do the same. To build a home where no one must perform in order to feel loved.

So, if you want to learn how to be a better mom, this isn't the book for you. I don't have any new tips or words of wisdom for you that you can't find in a book already on the shelf. But if you want to see yourself differently, away from the standards our culture has placed on motherhood today, then keep reading.

I don't have all the answers. My kids act like maniacs half of the time. The other half I act like a maniac, still trying to come to terms with this thing called motherhood.

If you're tired of trying, but end up tripping over your own expectations of yourself, then keep reading. My hope is that you will find a glimpse of Jesus in these pages. That you will lay down your guilt, your fears and your shattered dreams and find yourself leaning against Jesus' chest and hear the relentless beat of His love for you — whether you woke up at 5 a.m. to bake muffins from scratch and are patting yourself on the back at your success, or you slept in, walked out to cereal all over the floor and kids fighting as they declared their innocence and you returned to bed while Netflix babysat.

I'm going to give you permission to fly the coop, sweet mama. Just for a little while. Come with me for a bit. Let's go to the beach. I'll make you a drink, and we'll sit with our toes in the sand. No one will beg us to go swimming or build sand castles. No one will wonder why we don't want to be buried in the sand. We'll feel the wind on our faces and breathe in the salty sea air.

Whatcha drinking, luv? Can I make you a margarita? I'll even add a pretty little umbrella to it if you like. Do you hear those waves crashing? Can you hear the seagulls cry? Come on, let's go. I'll bring you back, I promise. And you don't even need to pack any bags.

The heart of Jesus beats for you, sweet mama. It beats with a love so deep and wild that if you lean against it long enough, you might actually just believe it. And I pray you can fly back to your coop, to your little flock, and bring them a mom who knows she's not a perfect mom, but a mom who is loved perfectly by God.

Chapter 1
And Then I Had Kids

A little girl sighs as the party begins. Broad-rimmed glasses frame her face. Her sun-kissed hair, streaked with signs of too much chlorine and too many perms, tumbles recklessly out of her self-made French braid. To the touch, the hair feels more like crispy curly fries than hair, but she feels beautiful in her oversized high heels and shoulder pads.

The table is set with the finest china tea set to be found for miles around. The dolls sit around the table, giggling with excitement. Silk dresses, sprinkled with delicate flowers, adorn their fragile frames. With lace trimmed around their collars and frozen smiles painted on their porcelain faces, they stare adoringly at the girl before them. The girl passes around the food, and all the children politely say thank you as the plate is passed. The little girl is their mother, their friend, their confidante. The dolls are her children, her joy, her pride — her everything.

They pray, they eat, they laugh. The bond they share together is unbreakable, their hearts melded together with a love deep and strong. The children get up, tell their mother she's wonderful and scramble off to play with each other. They are siblings, but they are best friends.

The little girl sighs again with both delight and longing. Someday this would all be real. Images of a perfect future parade across the landscape of her mind. Someday, the tea won't be just water. The cakes won't be plastic. The children won't be stiff and lifeless. Their eyes will really dance with joy. Their giggles will really fill the silence. It will all be real. She will really be their mom, and life will be complete.

The alarm goes off way too early. Groggily, I set the snooze button again, all of my aspirations of waking up early slipping away with the night sky. The pitter-patter resonating through the walls tells me that six little feet are already up and running around. Hungry bellies call. A fight erupts as someone accuses someone else of another heinous crime. Stealing. Lying. Hitting. Looking. It could be any one of these atrocities. The looking at each other is the one that seems to create the most havoc. Her plea for justice will assail me as soon as I enter the kitchen. Yet for some reason, my verdict is never good enough. Not being fair is one of my most recognized attributes. I sigh, looking at the clock to see how many more hours until bedtime. Only 12. I can do this.

I open the curtains, and my heart sinks at the sight of the street cloaked in a shroud of white. So much for getting all that energy out at the park. The drudge of winter settles deeper in my heart with every snowflake that falls. What I wouldn't give for a beach right now. What I wouldn't give for a margarita. Wait … should I be thinking about margaritas at 7 a.m.?

The kitchen greets me with three precious smiles and one giant mess. Cheerios blanket the floor. Milk lines the table. The voice in the back of my mind tells me that a good mom would have woken up earlier. A good mom, bright-eyed and smiling, would have risen with the dawn. A good mom would have prepared oatmeal for their tummies, devotions for their hearts and fresh-squeezed juice for their brains. But all I can see is that mess, which gives me one more thing to do on this snowy, dreary, same-as-every-other day.

My tea brews as the wind howls, its grip threatening to rip the house apart. Another fight erupts. This time the victim takes it upon herself to hand out justice. A good kick to the back ought to do it, she decides. I grip the counter and bite my tongue.

How many more hours?

Sometimes Curious George is a really good babysitter. He's free, and he doesn't ask any questions.

I crawl back to bed while George takes over downstairs.

In the eyes of a dream-hazed girl, motherhood spread out before me like a sparkling treasure just waiting to be discovered. The map to find this treasure was simple. Grow up, get married, have babies and live happily-ever-after. The thought that a man would love me enough to sweep me off my feet and marry me, and that our love would create a miracle of life, was the single greatest thing I thought could happen to me.

That girl with the green-streaked, perm-fried hair had big dreams for her future. From the time I could walk, I pretended to be a mom. For hours upon hours, I imagined what it would be like to be a mom, holding my babies, watching them grow, guiding them through the slippery slopes of life and throwing tea parties where everyone smiled and no one complained. Through my glittering gaze, I could imagine no greater life goal.

And then I had kids.

As I grew up, it didn't take long for me to realize that not all mothers are created equal. Perhaps my giant bi-focal glasses gave me an advantage to seeing things clearly. Either way, I deduced two things: There are good mothers, and there are bad mothers. I had a good mom. Not perfect, but she loved us well and gave of herself to give us more than we deserved. I felt loved, safe and hopeful. But even in the haven of my beautiful childhood, I built a standard around this sacred calling of motherhood. I had years to plan, so not surprisingly, I had a very cut and dry idea of what motherhood would look like.

I'm not alone. We all do this, whether we dreamed about it from the time we could walk, or not until the time we saw two lines on the pregnancy test. If we had a mom who appeared to be supermom or a mom who jumped ship, we all entered motherhood with two very important convictions.

There are things a good mom does. There are things a good mom doesn't do.

Although I don't know where it all stems from, I gave myself a pretty high standard as a mom. One, mind you, I fully intended to reach. I believed that a good mom makes her children the center of her world. She stays home, bakes cookies, makes food from scratch, is never unhappy, volunteers at the church and the school, stays in shape, reads to her children at night, plays catch, plays board games, makes elaborate crafts, wakes up before dawn, saves money, sews her kids' clothes and never longs for anything other than the blissful life of a mother.

A good mom doesn't pick her kids up late from dance. A good mom doesn't complain. A good mom doesn't sleep in. A good mom doesn't feed her kids frozen chicken nuggets. And above all … a good mom doesn't yell … under any circumstances.

And then I had kids.

You're probably smarter than me. You might be looking at my standard and thinking to yourself, *At least I'm not as crazy as this girl!* Touché. Regardless, even if you aren't crazy, you still probably entered motherhood with a standard that was shaped by how you were raised. Either you saw your mom and thought you needed to be just like her, or you looked at her and saw exactly what you didn't want to be. Or it was a combination of both. There were things you felt she did that were right, but some things you wanted to do differently.

Let's let our moms off the hook, though. This book isn't about our mother wounds. There are really smart psychologists who can help us out with that. They've written books with far more insight than I have.

Yes, we have mother wounds. And let's be honest — we probably gave our mothers a few wounds, as well. This book isn't about our moms, though, bless their hearts. This book is about us. The standards we made for ourselves, regardless of what impacted the shaping of that standard. The type of mom you thought you would be when you caressed your swollen belly and dreamed of holding that baby in your arms.

And then you had kids.

Here's the deal: Our standard for what makes a perfect mom works really well with porcelain dolls. They do what you want. They don't talk back. They hold china tea sets without breaking them and wear silk dresses without staining them. They say things like "please" and "thank you" and, "Mother, you are wonderful."

Kids — well, that's just it — kids are more, how do I say it? Kids are a bit more complicated. They cry. They whine. They spit out your dinner made from scratch. They bite the neighbors and run naked through the grocery store. They fight during family devotions and family vacations. They are ungrateful at Disneyland and cry at the beach. They keep you up at night and get sick at the most inconvenient times. And they're downright adorable, and we love them so much it feels like our hearts might explode.

This is what makes it all the more excruciating. We want to be good moms, because we love them! We want to give them the life we think they deserve. Not one mom I've ever met has told me she wakes up in the morning concocting a sinister plan for how she can ruin her children's lives. I know our kids think it. Which, by the way, I've just started agreeing with.

Yes, children. I want to make your life miserable. Yes, I think of all the ways I can fail you today.

But those words sink like bricks in my soul. If they only knew how many times I've thought of the ways I could fail them today. And how it breaks my heart.

Oh, sweet mama. I know you don't want to fail your kids. You want to get it right. You want to love them well. In fact, I can see right into that beautiful mind of yours and see that you do actually think of the ways you can fail your children. Because you think you already have.

You think you failed them yesterday when you fed them frozen pizza and canned green beans. You think you failed them when you sent them to bed last night without a bath. You think you failed them this morning when the whining shredded your eardrum into tiny fragments of insanity. You are certain you failed them when you lost it in the car and then watched their tiny bodies walk innocently through the school gate.

I know you don't want to fail your kids. I've sat next to you and heard your failures. I've looked into your eyes and seen your regret. I know it because I've lived it.

Motherhood is supposed to be the greatest job in the world, right? At least that's what others told us. That's what we tell ourselves. *Why can't I just get this so very important job right?* And we're bogged down with a guilt so heavy that it's pinned us right to the floor.

We want to be good moms! We want to get this thing called motherhood right. Yet, try as we might, we never seem to be able to reach the standard of excellence we think our children deserve. In the depths of night, when our minds play back the scenes of failure throughout the day, the guilt seeps through our veins, anchoring itself in our hearts.

Why did I yell over something so small? They're just kids. Why can't I be more patient? Why can't I get it right?

So we make promises.

Tomorrow, I won't yell. Tomorrow, I will be patient. Even when they fight and cry. I will be patient and gentle. I will be kind and soft-spoken. I will wake up early in the morning, have a quiet time and face the day with grace and peace.

And then we wake up to the reality that our kids don't fit into our perfect standard. They aren't porcelain dolls. They are living, breathing people with needs and opinions.

I could keep my cool if they didn't fight so much. I could wake up early if I wasn't awake all night with a sick baby. I could laugh at the future if I wasn't so doggone tired. I could play more games if they helped clean up. I could make healthier dinners if I wasn't just trying to survive the day.

Yes, my standard for the perfect mother works really well when my children are sleeping innocently in their beds. And then, while their eyelids flutter with dreams, I remember who I was going to be. And when I stare into the face of reality, I realize I didn't even come close.

The standard also works really well in the fantasyland of marriage. You know, the marriage you dreamed about when Prince Charming rescues Cinderella from her life of hardship, and they run off into the sunset of happily-ever-after? Yep. I know that's what you think when you wake up next to the incredible snoring, farting man beside you.

I adore my husband. He's creative, sensitive, understanding and compassionate. He loves me and my children well. He's also a man and a human. Yet, it still surprises me when he acts like a human man.

Sheesh, after all this time, don't you think he would have morphed into that guy on the white horse? He knows that's what I want. I really don't think I'm asking too much here.

Just like how I could be a good mom if it weren't for those kids, I could also be the best wife if it weren't for my husband. I know you've thought the same thing, even if you won't admit it.

But real life isn't a fantasy. Marriage is hard. It's riddled with pain. Addiction, finances, sickness — they take their toll until you wonder what happened to that bright-eyed girl full of hope for the future.

When you don't know how you're going to pay the mortgage, finding the energy to bake cookies fades with the morning sun. When your husband tells you he looked at porn on the internet, and the betrayal sinks like a knife in your heart, waking up before dawn isn't on the to-do list. *Waking up is the day's accomplishment.* When your man finds video games more interesting than you, and you've spent the day wiping up poop and spit-up and throw-up off the walls, the girl in the white dress walking down the aisle to her dream come true disappears and the Wicked Witch of the West takes her place. When morning sickness keeps you closer to the toilet than the oven, baking anything from scratch goes out the window. When postpartum depression eats away your joy, and you look at your baby with a horrified feeling of dread, making crafts on Pinterest loses its appeal. When a rambunctious child won't sit still long enough to learn to read, your dreams of raising the next Einstein crash to the ground. When the kids argue for the thousandth time over who cheated last in Monopoly, not raising your voice becomes a distant fairy tale.

This is reality. And most days, it isn't very pretty.

I don't know the sorrow your journey has brought you, but I do know it's real. But we don't talk about these very real issues that assail us every day as moms and wives. Instead, we post pictures on Instagram of how well we did — how amazing our kids are and how faithful our husbands are. And for some of you, this is real life. But for others, maybe your husband hasn't been faithful, and your marriage hasn't been blissful. Maybe, despite your best efforts, your kids haven't stopped fighting — and you've read every book, blog and article out there.

Yes, let's honor our kids and husbands. Yes, let's acknowledge our success. But first, let's redefine success, shall we? Is success really what we think it is? If so, then why do I see so many precious hearts laden with guilt? Why are so many beautiful, courageous women scared to death they aren't enough? When that voice whispers in your ear ... *Look at what she's doing ... Isn't she a good mom? ... Look at all the ways you've messed up today,* and you remember the mom you wanted to be, the only conclusion you can muster is that you must be a failure. After all, everyone else seems to be doing it right.

I am convinced that we live in a very difficult time as moms today. Even if you somehow made it to motherhood without a self-made standard, all you have to do is look around in order to find one.

All around us is a constant barrage of blogs, articles, books — all written by self-proclaimed experts — beating us over the head with *you should be doing this* and *you shouldn't be doing that* advice. Well-meaning friends and family members remind us of how kids should behave and how mothers should react. Unless we bury our heads and live in a hole, it's impossible not to perceive the standard that our culture screams in our faces.

Have you had enough? Are you tired of feeling like you aren't enough? Is it possible to live in freedom, free from the weight of guilt pinning you down?

Let's do it together. Let's be done with all this nonsense.

Did I mention yet that I was going to be the best mom ever? I was going to do it right. After all, how could someone who dreamed about this moment from the time she could walk get it wrong?

The girl with the crispy hair did grow up. After realizing perms are actually not all that attractive, she found the straightener, some chlorine-removing shampoo and a man who swept her off her feet. The fairy tale was finally beginning.

Ryan and I found out we were pregnant a little over a year after we were married. We were both still in school, dirt poor and madly in love. All I thought about the first year of marriage was how much more perfect life would be once a baby came along.

Don't we all know that a baby always makes things better?

When I saw those pink lines on the pregnancy test, my chest nearly burst with sheer ecstasy. The moment I had waited for my entire life dazzled before me.

When I held Selah in my arms for the first time, a joy unlike any other fell over me like shafts of sunlight after a storm. She entered this world as the sky groaned and wept in a summer torrent and stole my heart with a fierceness I didn't know was possible. My hands trembling with delight, I caressed her baby-soft skin, breathed in her baby scent and planned all the things we would do together.

And it was good. It truly was.

I loved being her mom, and I couldn't imagine a better way to spend my days. We lived in a small beach town in North Carolina. A house five minutes from the beach, friends with babies the same age — life was full and about as close to a fantasy as possible. I was a good mom, or so I thought. This was before Facebook, though, so I didn't have a way to know I was doing it all wrong. Jarred baby food for her belly, disposable diapers for her rear and Dora the Explorer for her brain.

As Selah grew, she fit perfectly into my good mom standard. I read "the" book, believed everything it told me my child should do, and *bam!* She did it! She rolled over at 4 months, crawled at 6 months and walked at 12 months. Right on schedule. She learned her alphabet at 18 months and knew her numbers at 20 months. She could sing every children's song I taught her before her 2-year-old birthday. Man, I was good! After all, my children's accomplishments and behavior is a direct reflection of my parenting success, isn't it?

On the outside, it appeared that I had everything figured out. No one saw the fear that paralyzed me in the shadows of night. No one saw the loneliness that followed me through my days. I didn't even let myself see the truth. I pushed it away, back into the shadows where uncomfortable thoughts belonged.

When you're 24 years old, an incredible mom and have the world figured out, it only makes sense that you should pack up and head to the sweltering jungle of Costa Rica as a missionary.

That's what we did. I didn't want to go. I liked my cookie-cutter life with my friends, my beach and my standard. But I thought that suffering for God would make me an even better mom, so I bit my tongue (well, let's be honest, I'm not very good at biting my tongue) and traipsed to a world of snakes, cliffs and mind-sucking heat.

When I say mind-sucking heat, I don't joke. When the air is that heavy with moisture, breathing is an act of labor. All energy goes to filling the lungs with enough oxygen to simply stay alive. With its turquoise ocean, dense rainforest and exotic wildlife, Costa Rica is a honeymooner's paradise.

It's a young mom's worst nightmare.

Our friends claimed we were living "the dream." Never in my dreams did the most poisonous snake in the world frequent my living quarters. In a place like this, nature controls people, not the other way around. The rainforest can't be contained. It inches into every crevasse; and left to its own devices, it will eventually take over anything in its path.

Six feet of rain in the month of October was only one of the obstacles we faced. With landslides, pot holes, deadly animals and no hospital for 30 miles, my mind raced with the endless possibilities of doom. Death literally lurked behind every corner. At least that's what my American-trained mind thought.

In fairness to my sweet baby girl heart, though, the mountain we drove over multiple times a month is actually called Cerro de la Muerte. Yes, that would be Mountain of Death. I must also point out that red lights are merely a suggestion in Costa Rica, and if you need to pass someone on the two-lane mountain highway of death, the fact that there are no guardrails is simply not something one considers. Needless to say, the fear I kept subdued in the safe suburbs of America couldn't hide in this untamed land.

When Selah was 18 months, I discovered I was pregnant again. What could be better than two babies under the age of 2, in the jungle, without a clue?

The morning sickness came. Ryan worked 16-hour days on top of the mountain while I remained in our 200-square-foot house waiting for the puma I knew was lurking just beyond the bushes. Did I ever see this puma? No. But I'm certain he was there, conjuring up a sinister plan to sink his teeth into my flesh.

Did I mention I don't speak Spanish?

The loneliness proved more than I could bear. My marriage floundered. My sanity wavered. Although I feared the fangs of a giant cat, it was the depression that eventually swallowed me whole. Going home was the only solution. I could only be a good mom back in the safety of America. So we headed home.

And so began the darkest days of my life.

Postpartum depression leveled me like wheat struck by the reaper's scythe. Our son, Gavin, entered this world with the same gusto he has lived with every day of his life, and while I loved him with all my heart, his birth catapulted me into the darkness of a deep, inescapable prison of depression. I tried to shake it. I prayed for it to flee. I worked harder to be a better mom. But my efforts only made me sink deeper and deeper into the abyss. If you haven't experienced it, then you won't understand that you can't simply snap your fingers and love your life. It takes over, like a poison, dripping into every aspect of life.

I looked around at my friends, comparing my feeble attempts at motherhood to theirs. On every level, my attempts paled in comparison. They all seemed happy and content as moms. They all seemed to thrive in their roles of tiny human development directors.

My poor babies. They deserve a better mom. A mom who knows what she's doing.

Despite my big dreams for motherhood, I clearly didn't know what I was doing. My baby didn't sleep through the night. My toddler didn't mind her manners. I stressed over the mess. I cried more than I laughed. I yelled more than I danced. All of the things I had looked forward to as a mom loomed before me, and I dreaded waking up each day. Instead of basking in the glorious destiny of motherhood, I sank deeper and deeper into the mire of disappointment. The hours dragged endlessly around the clock, towing my disillusioned heart with them. Staying at home with my children, living safe and snug within the haven of the American dream, was supposed to make me happy.

But as the walls of my home closed in around me, failure staring me straight in the face, I descended further into the dungeon of regret and shame. I tried to do better and be better. But no matter how hard I tried and how desperately I searched, I couldn't find the starry-eyed mama I thought I would be.

What do you do when life gets in the way of your expectations? I don't know what your journey looks like, sweet mama. But I know it's probably been hard. I know the way is bumpy and the valleys deep. I know the pain is real and the disappointment vast. How has life gotten in the way of who you thought you would be as a mom? How have you failed to live up to your own expectations of yourself? Have you ever stood before the chasm of despair, wondering where your dreams for your marriage and children went? Have you ever tried to climb out of the pit of hopelessness, only to fall back down more bruised and battered than before?

Oh, weary mama. I see you in that pit. I see your shattered dreams, your broken promises to yourself. I know. I've been there. In fact, I spent a good amount of time there.

I told you I used to be a really great mom.

And then I had kids.

But then I met Jesus.

Not the Jesus I thought I knew, the one shaking His finger at me in disgust. Not the Jesus who I thought hung His head in disappointment every time I wasn't the mom I thought I should be. No, I met a much bigger, much greater Jesus.

I met the real Jesus.

It began with the faintest sound of love, beating from a heart that bled love for me. And as I drew closer, it became the steady beat of a drum, the kind of beat that makes you want to get your dancing shoes on.

What do you do when you aren't the mom you want to be? What do you do when your kids, your husband and your life get in the way of the mom you thought you would be? Are we doomed to stay stuck in the shroud of our shortcomings? Or do we just throw in the towel and give up?

I don't want to wallow in my guilt anymore. I also don't want to give in to my anger. I love my kids too much. I know their hearts are on the line. I know *my* heart is on the line.

They say the time is short. It is. They say this job is important. It is. They say we only get one chance to get it right. They're right. But, what does that mean? How do we get it "right"? How do we make the most of this short, beautiful, crazy, mind-boggling, house-destroying, mountain-high-piles-of-laundry time?

I believe we need a shift of perspective. If we could learn to view our worth, our identity and our role as mothers from God's perspective, we could find freedom. Not freedom to fly the coop to crazy town whenever we feel like it. Not the freedom to beat ourselves upside the head, either. But a freedom that allows us to walk tall, knowing Whose we are and who we are.

The journey is hard, sweet mama. The stakes are high. But the God who loves you more than you can fathom is not finished with you.

In fact, this is just the beginning.

Digging Deeper

1. What are the expectations you place on yourself as a mom?

2. How many of these expectations were shaped by your childhood?

3. How many of these expectations were shaped by books, friends or blogs since you became a mom?

4. How has life gotten in the way of your expectations?

5. What makes you feel successful as a mom?

6. What makes you feel like a failure as a mom?

7. How does guilt impact you as a mom?

8. If you felt like you were enough, what would be different about your life?

Chapter 2

Practice Makes Perfect ... or Crazy

The living room floor went missing days ago, and I don't have the energy to go looking for it. The older two kids have been fighting incessantly for two weeks, and I've lost my temper too many times to count. The friend who left a message three weeks ago is still waiting, because I haven't found time to call back. The new neighbors moved in a month ago, and I still haven't walked the daunting 100 yards to shake their hands. The 7-year-old has been whining since May, and the grating drone is about to make me pull my hair out.

The mom who so desperately wanted to gather her chicks close has flown the coop, and the mom still here is a frustrated, worn out, short-on-time (and even shorter-on-patience) mess. If only Pinterest could see me now. She'd shake her crafty head in utter embarrassment. She does that, you know. Shakes her head at our feeble attempts at homemaking.

At least that's how a lot of us feel.

Lisa wants to be a good mom. She wants her kids to be smart, and she thinks if she sings the alphabet every night before they go to bed, she will succeed. Most days, she is successful. But other days, the moments slip by and she realizes that she rushed through bedtime and didn't take the time to sing such a simple song. In the silence of night, the guilt screams her name.

How could she let such a simple opportunity pass her by?

Her dreams for her children crash around her as she promises to do better tomorrow.

Sophie loves her kids. An unexpected pregnancy blessed her with two angels less than one year apart. She adores these little girls. Sometimes, she lets her kids watch TV in the car because the youngest cries in her car seat. She goes to Bible study, and her friends tell her how damaging it is for kids to watch TV. They talk about how kids just really need time with their mom. She goes home, dragging the chains of regret with her.

How does everyone else do it?

She loves her kids. She's doing her best. Clearly she isn't enough for this great calling. She just doesn't have what it takes.

Mollie is trying her best to juggle her roles of work and motherhood. Both seem to take more than they give. There are days when her kids need to entertain themselves because her responsibilities with work demand her attention. She read a blog today that told her all her kids need is her. They don't need nice things. They don't need fun experiences. They just need her, away from her phone and her computer. That's how they will know she loves them — by the amount of time she spends with them. Her work is tied to her phone, though. She has to be available in case a client calls. She tries to set boundaries. She loves her kids. She does spend time with them. But in the back of her mind, the pounding drum of her failure beats steadily throughout her day.

A good mom doesn't make her kids play outside by themselves.

A good mom would sit on the floor and play games.

A good mom would … her list goes on.

At the end of the day, she's certain she's disqualified from the "good mom" race.

What is your idea of the perfect mom? Be honest, because no one is looking at your heart right now except for you. Your list of the things a good mom does and doesn't do looks different from mine. Maybe you grew up in a home where your dad came home from work and put up his feet while your mom bustled around the kitchen catering to his every desire. This affects your perception of motherhood.

On the other hand, maybe you were raised by a single mom who worked a couple jobs to make ends meet. This impacts your view of motherhood.

Maybe you watched a friend's mom, thinking she had it all together, and in your mind, you believed that she embodied your perception of the mom you would strive to be.

What is your list? What is your standard? Was it shaped by someone in your life or someone you thought had it all together? Is it being shaped by a book you read recently or a blog you read every morning? None of these things are inherently bad. But when you look into your heart, if there is something you aren't doing that you think you should be doing, and you feel guilty because of it, that is your standard. If you pat yourself on the back when you do something and feel like you are successful as a mom, then that is your standard. We all have it because we're moms who love our kids. But we can't move forward until we've identified each of our own perceptions of perfection.

Living in Costa Rica as a missionary, I decided it was time to truly put my mothering skills to the test. Since a good mom should know how to sew, I decided to make some curtains for our little jungle home. I picked out the fabric, pulled out the sewing machine and prepared my husband to be utterly amazed.

First, let's talk about the fabric itself. Bright blue? Seriously? And the fact that I felt the need to pack my unused sewing machine in one of the 30 boxes we took to Costa Rica shows exactly how off my rocker I was.

It took days to hem those curtains.

For a beginner, I probably picked the worst kind of fabric. It pulled the opposite direction I wanted it to go, and my inexperienced hands didn't know how to bring it back under my control. The result was a very jagged, very ugly hem. On bright blue curtains. I was proud, though.

I held them up for Ryan to admire. And he did. He praised my efforts. He lied about the quality, commenting on my truly remarkable skills. Then, he asked for the extra fabric. I showed him the stash.

I laughed to myself, thinking, *Oh, sweet man. If only you knew how difficult this sewing business really is.* I practiced my look of delight so he wouldn't feel bad by his efforts.

Fifteen minutes later, he held up the dress he made for our daughter. Perfect hems lined an adorable bright blue dress that fit Selah perfectly. My expression of delight morphed into horror. Needless to say, I felt like an intruder on this thing called motherhood. How dare I impede on a territory I clearly had no right to claim?

There's nothing wrong with sewing curtains. I applaud all you talented women out there who can actually direct a piece of fabric in a straight line. You are superbly talented. Lately I've been thinking about pulling the sewing machine out and trying again. I'm sure Ryan will practice his look of delight, as well.

That sewing machine traveled back with me to two houses in North Carolina and three different houses in Colorado. Even after it broke, I held on to it, thinking one day I would figure it out. I tried making Selah a dress about a year after we returned from Costa Rica. I was sure if she wore it to church, everyone would be so amazed, and I would have orders coming in in no time at all. I could solve our financial problems and my failures as a mom at the same time!

Selah cried because the dress dug into her shoulders. The orders never came in. But I just simply couldn't let go of the idea that one day I would be a good mom, and somehow it would involve the sewing machine.

The problem wasn't the sewing. I know lots of moms who sew adorable clothes for their kids. Some of these moms have thriving businesses. Others do it just for fun. There's nothing wrong with sewing. The problem was that I placed an expectation on myself that didn't need to be there.

I was never taught how to sew. I never wanted to sew. I thought I was supposed to sew because that's what a good mom does. And then I stunk at sewing. To my young, scared-to-death-of-failing heart, failing at something I assumed was part of motherhood made me a failure as a mom. I looked around at other moms who seemed to succeed in areas where I failed, and in comparison I simply didn't measure up. Everyone else seemed to do this mothering thing better than me. Everyone else appeared to have it all together, while I unraveled at the seams.

I also thought that a good mom baked cookies with her children. It sounds so sweet in theory. We all put on our cute aprons, and we stare adoringly into one another's eyes as the eggs and flour and sugar magically make their way into the bowl. Um … is it really that hard to get the egg in the bowl? Does the counter have a magnetic power that causes the spoon to repel the bowl and splatter across it? Does the floor have an innate force that chocolate chips cannot resist?

It's better now that my kids are older, I will admit. But those years when they were little, baking cookies sent me spiraling into a deep hole that took weeks to recover from.

"Make memories," they said. "Don't worry about the mess," they said. "They" apparently never had to clean chocolate chips out of carpet. Yes, for our family, baking cookies was all about making memories. Memories burned into their little minds of Mom crying and everyone sent to timeout.

Memories … that's what we made.

And yet, despite the tears, despite the chaos, what did we keep doing? Baking freaking cookies. Why?

Because that's what a good mom does.

The problem wasn't the cookies. I have a friend who absolutely loves baking cookies with her kids. She embraces the mess and loves every second of the chaos. The problem was the standard. I thought I needed to bake cookies with my kids in order to be a good mom. Regardless of the fact that it actually turned me into the opposite of who I wanted to be.

It isn't just our own ideas that create this standard for what makes a perfect mom. The culture we live in has placed incredible expectations on us. I am convinced we live in one of the hardest times of history as moms. Not because of how bad the world is getting, but because the responsibility for all the problems our kids will face falls on the shoulders of us as moms. It's up to us to ensure our children's safety, success and happiness in life. In years past, kids were allowed to explore the world on their own, make mistakes, experience loss and disappointment and discover the cruel reality that life simply isn't fair. Today, however, it is expected that a mother keeps her children from experiencing any of this. She should ensure that her children never feel bored, excluded, unimportant, unvalued — or feel any pain or disappointment whatsoever.

And we wonder why we're tired.

In this information age, we are bombarded with research and statistics. We are told that the food we feed our kids is killing them. So we feed them more fruits and vegetables. But then we're told that just regular fruits and vegetables are full of poison. So we buy organic. But then we are told we are spending too much money, so somehow we are supposed to keep buying healthy food without spending any money. We aren't supposed to wear sunscreen because it's full of toxins, but the stares we get over a sunburned kid could kill. We're supposed to let our kids be kids but never let them act out in public. One expert tells us that private school is the only way to go. Another tells us if we're not homeschooling, we're ruining our kids. While another tells us we're fools to even consider anything other than a particular charter school. It's enough to make you crazy!

We are told not to care about how we look. We should be content with our bodies, because they bore our sweet little angels. Our stretch marks are love marks, and we should embrace them as beautiful. But then another article tells us how much our kids need to see their mom healthy and happy.

"Do it for your kids," they say.

Sorry, but what am I doing for my kids again? Besides feeding them, caring for them, spending all my money and every waking second on them? Oh, yeah, I'm supposed to find time to exercise without a gym membership because that would waste money, and without time away from my kids because that would be selfish, and by eating the healthy, organic food that doesn't cost any money. Oh, yeah, no problem!

Let's set the record straight, though. If I'm going to bust my butt at the gym and eat rabbit food all day, it's going to be for me!

We are told not to care about how the house looks.

They say, "Oh, you'll have laundry forever, but your kids are only young once."

Um, don't my kids need clean underwear while they are young? I can't tell you how many times I chose not to do the dishes and played Candyland instead, only to wake up the next morning with a sink full of dishes. And then I was standing at the sink, cursing Candyland because I had twice as many dishes to clean. Who do these people think will do my dishes if I don't do them? Who will do my laundry? I haven't met the fairy who does these jobs while I'm sleeping, so I guess until she shows up, it will continue to fall on me.

It's impossible to meet these standards our culture thrusts upon us. We try our best, but when we look around at all the articles, blogs, books and ghastly stares, we realize how short we measure up and how miserably we have failed.

Sweet mamas, we have a problem on our hands. We all want to be good moms. We want to be the best moms for our children. I know that YOU want to be the best mom for your kids. You want to give them everything good in this world and more. The problem is that we've misunderstood what it means to be a good mom. We've let our imaginations and the culture we live in define what a good mom looks like. And what we have is a standard that's impossible to reach.

This standard that we've convinced ourselves we must reach in order to be a good mom, combined with real life, is a recipe for disaster. Instead of enjoying the precious little time we have as moms, we're burnt out, miserable, guilt-ridden wrecks. I can almost guarantee that you've not done all the things you said you were going to do as a mom, and you've done the things you said you'd never do as a mom.

And the guilt is killing you.

We all want to be good moms. That isn't the problem. We know that being a mom is the greatest job in the world! But as I talk with moms and listen to their hearts, I see more guilt than joy. I see more fear than hope. I see more insecurity than courage. This is not what motherhood should be about.

So, what went wrong?

We know we're supposed to enjoy it. We know they're only little once. We know the days will pass like shifting shadows, and we will wonder what we did with all that time.

I could chalk this up to my own craziness. Maybe it really is just me — I got my calling wrong. I'm just not cut out for this mothering gig. I thought this for a long time. But like the stories of the moms at the beginning of this chapter, I know I'm not alone. I've heard so many stories from moms brave enough to offer me a glimpse of their hearts. Not the glamorous glimpse of perfection. But the beautiful, heartbreaking glimpse of reality.

What's your story? When do you feel like you are an imposter on this grand calling of motherhood? When do you feel that you just simply don't measure up to everyone around you, and the mom up the street or across the table would do a much better job? And you're convinced the mother across the table would agree with you?

How do we enjoy the moments when the days feel like eternity? Why are we walking around weighed down by guilt rather than dancing with delight that we get to bear this awesome burden of raising a flesh and blood, air-breathing person?

Because we are so scared we've failed. Failed our kids. Failed God.

Those days when I lost it baking cookies, I pictured God shaking His head in such disappointment. *Girl, get it together! I gave you these kids, and this is how you treat them? How hard is it to play Candyland? I should have given these kids to someone else. Someone who would do a better job.*

And guilt cloaks me like a mantle.

Even more than the reality that I was a disappointment to myself and my kids, I felt, when face to face with staggering evidence, that I was a disappointment to God. He entrusted these precious hearts to me, and I failed Him. Daily. I begged for forgiveness, promising to do better the next day. Although I knew my position in Heaven never changed, I was certain His feelings for me changed as often as I failed.

Do you ever feel like you've disappointed God? Do you ever feel like He's shaking His head at you, wishing He had given your kids to someone else? And in some ways, this feels good. We like conviction, don't we? We like to feel bad about ourselves because that's how we change, right? We hear a sermon or read a blog about how important the role of a mother is to her children, and the truth stares us right in the face with a proof we can't deny that, despite our best efforts, we simply don't measure up. And for some narcissistic reason, we feel better when we feel bad. When we wallow in regret, it makes us feel that in some way we've paid for our mistakes. I don't know if it's different for you, but no amount of guilt ever made me not lose my temper. No amount of shame ever made me love Candyland.

Oh, sweet mama, is there another way? Is it possible to really let go of the standard? I know we all long for it. Will more guilt help us to become the moms we so desperately want to be? Can we stop striving for the impossible standard we are all trying to meet? We talk about how we long to be free from it — how it eats away our joy and robs our time. But if your day is dictated by your guilt, then you are not walking in freedom. If you read something that someone else is doing, and now you feel like you must do it, then you are letting the standard rule both your heart and your home.

The problem isn't all the little things that we think we should be doing. It's good to feed our kids healthy food, I'm not denying that. They need to be nurtured and loved well. Candyland is not the devil. Chutes and Ladders is a different story, however, as we all know. Sewing curtains, baking cookies, singing the alphabet and playing games are good things. Magical summer experiences are opportunities for a family to draw closer together, creating memories that will last a lifetime.

I'm not suggesting that we stop caring — or leave our kids to their own devices. I know what those little gremlins are capable of ... it wouldn't be pretty.

I'm also not suggesting that we stop doing anything we think a good mom would do. I could sit around all day and drink margaritas, basking in my freedom from guilt, but is that what motherhood is about?

I know the moments matter.

I know little hearts matter.

How do we make the most of the moments, when the days feel like they will never end? How do we rise up out of the ashes of guilt and walk in the fullness of our rich calling as moms?

That's the question this book seeks to answer, and I can tell you from hard-won experience that the answer doesn't lie in trying harder.

But there is an answer.

It came to me in the depths of my own failure. When I couldn't see straight because I was so dizzy from trying, God reached out and pulled me close to His chest. At first, I fought Him, like a toddler throwing a temper tantrum. As my Father held me tightly in His arms, assuring me of His presence while I kicked and screamed, I couldn't give up. Tight-fisted and stiff-backed, I beat against His chest in frustration. Until I had nothing left to give. And like that toddler who realizes her daddy isn't going to let go, I finally let myself go limp in His arms.

He held me, and as my cries faded, I heard His gentle whisper.

"Shhhh. I've got you, sweet one. I'm here. You don't have to be afraid anymore. Shhhh. It's okay. You're safe now. I'm here."

"But, God!" I cried. "I've messed up so much. I'm not the mother I thought I would be."

"How about you stop trying to be a good mom, and I'll show you what a big God I am," came His tender reply.

And that's when I heard it. The beat of His heart so fervent, so beautiful, so wild ... beating for me.

Can I say it again to you, worn and tired mama? As you try to love your kids well and feel that everything you do is never enough, can I tell you again? The heart of Jesus beats love for you. Not shame. Not disappointment. But love.

Maybe we've had God's love all wrong. Isn't He pleased when we do the right thing? And disappointed when we fail? Doesn't He want us to live up to the promises we make in the still of night when we remember just how far we've fallen?

What if that isn't how God thinks at all? What if He's not at all surprised when we fail at our feeble attempts of perfection? What if He is so madly in love with us that His feelings don't change based on our behavior?

And — wait for it — what if it's actually *His love* that changes us, not our attempts at trying harder? What if, by realizing how incredibly loved we are, we actually started living like it?

Don't believe me? Let me show you. This is Paul's prayer for you in the book of Ephesians.

"May you have the power to understand, as all God's people should, how wide, how long, how high and how deep His love is.

May you experience the love of Christ, though it is too great to understand fully. Then you will be made complete with all the *fullness of life and power* that comes from God."[1]

Fullness of life and power. Doesn't that sound refreshing?

Power to stay calm in the midst of chaos. Power to forgive those who have wounded us. Power to keep our mouths closed when we want to shout.

Fullness of life. No more striving for worth. No more straining for attention. Completely and lavishly satisfied.

But how? Reading our Bible more? Memorizing Scripture? That will help us remember, but the power doesn't come from the doing.

Where then? Baking more cookies? Reading more blogs? Nothing wrong with either, but that's not where this power comes from.

May you experience the LOVE OF CHRIST, though it is too great to understand fully.

This is where the power comes from. This is where we will be made complete ... full ... free. Free from the comparisons. Free from our anger, our impatience and our selfishness. Guilt and shame have no power to change us. It is in being loved that we are changed.

Author and blogger Sarah Bessey puts it this way: "Living loved, we relax our expectations, our efforts, our strivings, our rules, our breath, our plans, our job descriptions and checklists; we step off the treadmill of religious performance. We are not the authors of our redemption. No, God is at work, and His love for us is boundless and deep, wide and high, beyond all comprehension."[2]

We've been trained to fight it, though. Trained to deny it, because it must be too good to be true, right? It feels so much more spiritual to beat ourselves up. It feels so much more holy to remind ourselves how short we've fallen from God's glory instead of claiming the verse that says, in Christ, we now share in His glory![3]

You may believe that God loves you because He's God and He has to. But do you believe He likes you? Do you believe He's fond of you — that you take His breath away? Is God someone you approach with fear, or is He your Abba — the Daddy whose arms hold you safe? Do you hear a voice of judgment looming over you, or do you hear Him rejoicing over you with singing?

Last year, Ryan and I traveled to the war-torn country of Rwanda. One day, we visited a local orphanage in the capital city. Despite the language barrier, we played and laughed with the children. All people understand the language of love, and for one afternoon, love built a bridge across an ocean of differences. Children of all ages ran around us, stealing our hearts and wrecking our small view of God.

Toward the end of the afternoon, we entered a room filled with children who couldn't run around and play with the others. In this room, the nannies cared for the children with special needs — those weakest but certainly not forgotten. We held these angels, and our hearts nearly burst with anguish at their plight.

One boy in particular caught my attention. During our entire stay, he wouldn't stay still. Through groans and cries, he tried to communicate, but the words couldn't find the pathway from his brain to his lips. I tried holding him, but he fought me. Arching his back and flailing his arms, he tried to escape my embrace. As if fighting a battle seen only by his eyes, he pushed and kicked. My heart lurched as I watched him fight — watched him thrash against me.

Just as I was about to give up, I remembered my babies back home — the times they fought against me in frustration and anger. And I held that precious boy even closer. I began to sing the songs I sang over my children. Lullabies that soothed their hearts. Promises that calmed their minds. As I sang over him, his stiff body softened. His groans subsided, and with a sigh that needed no translation, he fell limp against my chest.

Sweet mama, did you know your Abba rejoices over you with singing? He delights in you. Zephaniah 3:17 says, "The Lord your God is with you, the

Mighty Warrior who saves. He will take great delight in you; in His love He will no longer rebuke you, but will rejoice over you with singing."[4]

It's a song of hope. It's a song of truth. And at its very heartbeat, it's a song of love.

Will you let yourself fall limp against His chest so you can hear it?

Author Brennan Manning says, "Define yourself radically as one beloved by God. This is the true self. Every other identity is illusion."[5]

It's radical to define yourself as God's beloved. It doesn't feel natural to claim this as who we truly are. But until you see yourself as a child of God, forgiven and set free, you will keep striving for perfection. You are a daughter of the King, luv! He's spun you into gold. The problem is, we still think we're only straw. So we spin and spin, trying to spin straw into gold. When all along, the gold is already there!

What if we stopped wasting time trying to spin straw into gold and started living as gold? What if, in the face of grace, we saw ourselves as God's beloved? What if we stopped spinning for perfection and believed that we're okay just the way we are? We would rise up. In freedom. In hope. In truth. Ready to take this same grace into our world.

So why are we stuck in our guilt? Why are we weighed down with shame? I believe it boils down to the fact that many of us have a false view of God and a false view of ourselves. Once we begin to see our worth, our identity and our role as mothers from God's perspective, we can let go of the standard. Because, even though we think the standard is perfect, it's really simply the status quo.

I want more than that for my children. I want more than that for my marriage. I want to fly the coop of perfection and fall desperately in the arms of Jesus.

Will you fly with me?

Digging Deeper

1. In what ways do you disappoint yourself as a mom?

2. What are the promises you make to yourself at the end of the day for how you will do it better tomorrow?

3. Do you feel like you've disappointed God?

4. How do you think God views you right now?

5. Do you feel like His feelings change when you meet your standard?

6. Do your feelings for yourself change whether or not you've met your standard?

7. Does the idea that God is not disappointed in you feel wrong?

8. Do you remind yourself more that you have fallen short of God's glory or that, in Christ, you now share in His glory?

Chapter 3
And Oh, How They Cheered

I wake up in the early morning, the sun's rays peeking through the window-pane, tendrils of light enveloping me with a warm embrace. The glow beckons me to a new day, a new opportunity. Some mornings I am more grateful for God's new mercies than others. I open my Bible, letting the words pour over my weary soul. Today will be different. Today I will get it right.

I walk out of my room, a skip in my step, ready to face the day. Their little faces smile up at me, and I shower them with kisses. I'm so lucky to get to stay home with them. My heart swells with gratitude, and I want to freeze this moment in time forever.

We make it through breakfast. My smile is real. My peace is secure. I send them to brush their teeth. We're on a roll. We just might make it out the door without a fight.

I speak too soon. Someone screams from upstairs. I rush up the stairs, certain to find blood, a gash through the skin — something deadly. No, someone won't share the toothpaste. Apparently screaming seemed like the appropriate response in the child's mind. I keep my cool. *Today I'm not going to lose it.* I tell them gently to work it out and head back downstairs when the second scream jolts me from my dreamy haze.

Seriously, what happened this time?

It's worse than I thought. Someone is standing in someone else's room, giving motherly advice. My patience flies out the window. My heart starts to race. How can a moment change so quickly? How can my peace flee in an instant?

I lock myself in the bathroom where they can't find me. The pounding on the door comes seconds later.

"Mom, she won't listen."

"Mom, she's being mean."

"Mom, why don't you ever listen to me?"

I open my phone, seeking solace in the comforting reality of Facebook. After all, don't I always feel better after seeing the best of other people's lives? I scroll through the posts, and one word screams louder than the kids on the other side of the door.

FAILURE!

One friend made blueberry muffins for breakfast. Another friend posted a picture of her snuggling in bed with her kids. Still another posted a picture of flowers her husband brought her. No reason, just because he loves her. I know my husband loves me. But he didn't bring me flowers. Jealousy inches its way through my veins, fastening its deadly grip around my heart. The smiles on my screen send a thousand tiny daggers into my conscience.

I was going to get it right today. Today was supposed to be different. I was going to keep my cool, guard my tongue and enjoy the moment. But I'm locked in the bathroom, kids pounding on the door, late for school, wishing I could go back to bed — and it's only 9 a.m.

Our promises to ourselves always seem attainable in the quiet of night.

And then we wake up and remember we have kids.

When I was in high school, I ran track and cross-country. At the beginning of the track season of my senior year, one of my coaches told me that if I tried hard enough, I could break the school record for the two-mile run. So began a grueling season of training. All I needed to do was beat my PR (personal record) at every race, and at the state meet, I would meet my goal. I poured every ounce of my energy into getting faster. I learned to ignore the pain, deny the belief that I couldn't go one more mile, couldn't go one second faster. Mind over matter.

I learned to convince my stomach that it didn't really feel as if it would give me back my lunch. My legs didn't really feel like bricks dragging through sludge. I got to the point where I could convince my brain to ignore the need to go to the bathroom. Just for the record, your brain might think one thing, but at some point, your body decides the brain actually doesn't know what it's talking about. It didn't matter, though. Wetting my pants simply became par for the course.

Every race shaved a few more seconds off my time. And oh, how my team would cheer.

As the season progressed, my goal became the team's goal. Hurdlers suddenly cared about the long-distance races. They watched and cheered by the side of the track. I became a mascot of hope. Not because I won every race, but because I was fighting for more than 1st place. I was fighting for the place deep inside each of us that believes dreams really can come true. Even the pole vaulters turned with bated breath to watch the clock, anticipating the time it would reveal. In case you didn't know, pole vaulters aren't known for their concern during those long, boring races at the end of a track meet. But oh, how they cheered now!

Despite anemia, several bouts of strep throat and an almost failed trigonometry class, the state meet arrived. I was more than ready. All the training, the pain and the sacrifice culminated in this one moment — the moment when I would go home either the victor or the loser against the clock. It was now or never. I would never get the chance again to prove my ability.

The gun blasted, and I flew, confident in my ability and pace. I knew exactly the time I needed to register around each lap. I didn't care what place I was in, it was the time that mattered. With legs like rubber and lungs like fire, I sprinted the last 200 yards, crossing the finish line eight seconds faster than the previous record.

And oh, how they cheered.

Today, I scrubbed vomit out of the carpet. Nobody cheered.

Yesterday, I cleaned poop off the wall. Nobody cheered.

Last night, I stayed up late baking cookies for a class party. Nobody cheered.

Last week, I spent the day riding a bus to the butterfly pavilion with 60 screaming second-graders. The headache I came home with lasted for three days. Nobody cheered.

I wash dirty underwear and socks several times a week. Nobody cheers. I wash the clean underwear and socks several times a week because certain children think the laundry basket is a drawer. Nobody cheers.

I give and clean. And clean and give. And give and give. And then clean some more.

Nobody cheers.

I don't know about you, but nobody cheers for me as I go throughout my days as a mom. I know Ryan appreciates what I do as a mom, and I keep holding out for the day my kids will, too, but it just isn't the same as the cheering crowd screaming their thrill at my accomplishments. Before I became a mom, I was able to measure my worth based on my accomplishments. Do well in school — get good grades. Train hard for a race — beat the record. Work hard at my job — get a raise.

For some reason, my children haven't learned this simple arithmetic lesson. Clean the house — house stays clean. Ask to put clothes away — clothes get put away. Spend all afternoon making dinner — children eat food and tell you that you're wonderful. Maybe it's different in your home, but this is not the case in mine.

What actually happens is this. It's morning. Again. We're getting ready for school, but we could be getting ready to go anywhere. The scene is the same, regardless of the destination. We're usually running late. I've told you I have this dilemma with getting up early.

"Go get your shoes on."

Ten minutes later, I call up the stairs, "It's time to go; do you have your shoes on?"

A surprised face appears at the top of the stairs. "No."

"Why not?"

"I don't know."

"We gotta go! How many times do I have to tell you to put your shoes on? It's not like we ever leave the house without shoes on. It happens every day. The same thing. We put our shoes on and leave the house."

I run to the bathroom to brush my teeth. Stinky breath isn't a problem if we make it in time to drop them off outside the school. But if we're late, I have to go inside and sign them in. I have to at least appear as if I didn't just roll out of bed.

I hear the sound of piano keys drifting through the house.

"Who is playing the piano? Do you have your shoes on?"

"Oh, whoops. I forgot."

We're in the car. We just might make it.

"Mom, what's for dinner?"

"Chicken pot pie."

"Oh." I can hear the disappointment dripping from that one word.

"Mom, did you sign my folder?"

"Mom, did you sign my permission sheet for the field trip?"

"Mom, I have a report due tomorrow. Can you go to the store and buy everything I need for it? I HAVE to have it done tonight."

"Why didn't you tell me sooner?"

"I forgot."

Have I mentioned that I love these kids with every ounce of my being? I love being their mom. But there isn't a lot of affirmation that I'm getting it right. No one tells me I'm doing a good job. Most of the time there's more laundry I haven't folded. More dishes I haven't washed. More projects I haven't finished. And more behavior problems I haven't solved.

And then I look around at how well all the other moms are doing.

I know deep down we all have problems. I know nobody's life is perfect. I know this deep down somewhere in the caverns of my being. I guess I just forget. Sounds like someone else I know. Apparently the apple doesn't fall far from the tree.

I've joined moms' groups for support. I've read blogs and books and articles. Unfortunately, other moms are often our worst critics. We judge each other. We compare ourselves to each other. We sit around and tell each other how to do it and then go home feeling worse than before. I look around at everyone else, comparing myself and always coming up short. My conclusion is simple.

Do more. Do what she's doing. Do what the experts suggest. Perform well, and they will cheer. Try harder, and they will applaud.

But most of the time, the crowd is silent. And the voices in my head that say I'm not enough scream louder than the whining children outside the bathroom door.

I thought I knew who I was before I became a mom. I was successful, smart and talented. Did that all disappear the day my baby arrived? Or did that woman who felt worth something leave the day Mama became my name?

We all need to feel like we're worth something. We might look for worth in different things, but I've found as moms, we tend to look in similar places. The most common place is in performance. Our performance as moms, our children's performance and our performance outside our homes.

Our Performance as Moms

"You're such a good mom."

A simple phrase that washes over us like rain pouring down on a sun-cracked desert. Words that heal. Words that refresh. Words that give us the strength to carry on one more day.

Words that make us hungry for more.

It feels good to be told we are doing a good job. We need it, and we should tell every mom we encounter each day that she is doing a good job. But it never satisfies. We always want more. Maybe I did a good job today, but what about tomorrow? What will I have to offer the world tomorrow?

I love Facebook. I feel that it has a place in a world where people move away and it's hard to stay in touch. But Facebook is full of mamas looking for worth. I see it in the pictures of their homemade valentines straight off of Pinterest. I see it in their pictures of homemade dinners. I see it in the pictures of crafts and activities that fill their days.

It's not just on Facebook. It's at the tables in our support groups. It's in our Bible studies and playdates. Moms smiling. Children posing. And behind the smiles, I see their mama hearts, crying out for someone to tell them they are doing a good job. *Somebody tell me that I matter! Somebody tell me that my efforts aren't in vain. Somebody tell me that cleaning vomit out of carpet and poop off walls is something to applaud. Somebody see that my days aren't passing by into oblivion without purpose. Look at this dinner I made from scratch. Look at my accomplishments today. And tell me that this thing they call motherhood really is worth it.*

And sometimes the crowd cheers.

We hear their applause. *Good job, mama. You matter. You are seen. You are worth something. We see your efforts, and we applaud your performance.*

Other times, though, the crowd is silent. They don't see the tears behind the smiles and the mess behind the camera. They didn't see the fighting while you baked those adorable Easter cookies or hear the whining over having to eat your delicious meal. When the cheers fade and we are alone in the silence of our homes and the hollow space in our hearts, we are forced to stare face to face with the fact that, despite our best efforts, our satisfaction is fleeting. Our worth is no more than sand slipping through our fingers. Because tomorrow someone else will do something better. Someone else will win the good mom award.

More, our hearts cry out. *Do more. Try harder. Perform better.*

Our Children's Performance

It's only a matter of time, though, that despite our best efforts, we realize that our performance just simply isn't enough. So we turn to our children, living vicariously through their success. I feel really good about myself when my kids behave well. After all, it must be some reflection of my incredible mothering skills.

A few weeks ago, we were eating lunch at a favorite Mexican restaurant. An older man came up to our table, informing us that he had taken care of our bill because our family was so sweet and our children so well behaved. *Great job, kids. You came through for me this time!* I felt like I had somehow tapped into the treasure vault of the mysteries of motherhood.

Somehow I had figured out this parenting thing, and someone noticed.

This is not the norm, however. I have been the mom whose child hits the other kids at the park. I've been the mom whose child pushed another child down the stairs. I've been the mom whose child punched a hole in a friend's door. I've been the mom who drug her child through the grocery store while he kicked and screamed in fury.

My incredible mothering skills seem somewhat faded in times like these.

There is an incredible amount of pressure today for our kids to be successful. It begins the day they are born. A child who is successful at grabbing hold of a nipple means the mother is successful. If not — if they struggle — there must be something wrong. If a child rolls over before the correct age, his or her achievement is praised. But should the child be late, somehow that makes the mother feel as if she's doing something wrong.

Oh, we say it doesn't matter. We say every child is different, and that's okay. But when we sit around our tables and homes, we can't help but compare our children. A friend's child is reading at 3. Yours is 7 and couldn't care less. Another mom claims her child was potty trained at 12 months. You're convinced your child will walk down the aisle still in diapers.

Somehow we've convinced ourselves that successful children means a successful mom. This is true to some extent. Obviously reading to our kids does help with learning. Playing games helps cognitive thinking. Healthy food helps brain function. But it's become so extreme, we feel guilty if our child is behind in any area. We don't want them to be left out, or better yet, we don't want ourselves to be left out of the I'm-better-than-you game.

So we push. We strive. We run from activity to activity. Don't you want to be the best piano player? Don't you want to be the best soccer player? And when the crowd cheers, our hearts swell with pride. I must have done something right. I must be worth something. Look at my kids! Look at their accomplishments.

Their performance makes us feel better about ourselves. We compare ourselves to other moms. We compare our kids to other kids. And one way or another, we convince ourselves that either we truly are better, or we've come up short again. When they fail, we feel like failures. When they act out in public, we want to run and hide. When they fight while another family sits across the restaurant holding hands, we wonder where we went wrong. When they scream through Hobby Lobby, and everyone in the store gives you a look of death, we wish we could crawl into a hole and disappear.

It's me. I'm not doing anything right. Why can't these kids behave? What am I doing wrong? There must be something wrong with me. These kids deserve better than me. Look at those kids. Look at that mom. She is such a good mom. My kids would be better off with her.

And it isn't completely our fault. Just the other day I read an article written by a prominent Christian leader. He said that our children's behavior is directly related to our parenting. A child who is respectful reveals parents who are doing their job. This article didn't talk about the moms who pour tears at night over a child who is struggling with respect. This article didn't mention the shame moms feel when their kids fight in public. It didn't say anything about the sticker charts, devotions, Bible memorizing efforts so many moms are giving with little results. All this article did was throw a heaping dose of shame down the throats of the moms who are already choking on their own convictions.

While I agree that my parenting shapes my children, if my children's choices are completely correlated to my parenting, then I'm raising robots, not human beings.

My children are lost without Jesus.

My children are desperate for the same grace that sets me free. They will walk a road that I haven't walked. They will make choices that I cannot make for them. And they will one day come face to face with the option to either choose grace or choose their own way. I will walk this road with them. But I cannot choose for them. I can guide them to the truth, but I cannot force the truth into their hearts.

But it's hard. It's hard when I'm surrounded by lies disguised as truth.

I want my kids to make the right choices.

But am I more concerned with how other people will view me because of those choices than I am with their hearts finding freedom in the unfathomable love of Jesus?

Do their poor choices make me feel that I have failed?

When my kids tell a stranger about the real meaning of Christmas, do I beam with pride?

When they fight in the street, am I more concerned with what the neighbors will think than I am about the state of their hearts?

We're hungry for more. More praise. More applause. More hope.

And we're notorious for finding it in the wrong places.

Our Performance Outside Our Homes

I learned fairly quickly in my journey as a mom that my kids weren't going to make me feel really great about myself. I discovered a much better way to hear the cheering crowd.

I found it in ministry.

Several years ago, I began writing and teaching. I led mission trips and taught Bible studies at my church. I taught from my vault of wisdom, knowledge and experience (I hear you snickering). Want to know the crazy part? People listened. I started speaking at other churches, retreats and gatherings. For some wild reason, women came, they listened and they didn't throw tomatoes. In fact, they showered me with praise. And in their praise, I found worth. People wanted to hear my words. They took notes on my wisdom. Finally, I had found some people who understood the math equation. I spend time preparing a talk + you come and listen and tell me how great I am = I feel good about myself. It was perfect. I thrived on their compliments.

I also discovered I had a very deep problem.

When they praised, I rose to the heights of happiness. When they were silent, I fell into the depths of worthlessness. And that voice that loves the silence crept in once again to whisper lies in my ear.

Not enough. Never enough.

In what ways do you perform outside your home? I am wildly awed by the courageous women who raise kids and work full time. Whether by choice or by circumstances, I am astounded by their strength — and their ability to wake up so early. This book isn't about whether or not we should be working moms or stay-at-home moms. This is, however, about the pressure we face as moms to be everything in every way.

While no one would openly deny the importance of shaping the character of small human beings within the walls of our homes, there is increasing pressure to do more than simply stay at home (although we all know there's nothing simple about this job). Again, I understand that not everyone is fortunate enough to have a choice in this matter. The pressure is real, though, regardless of the need.

We are told, directly and indirectly, to do more — be more — make more. Not surprisingly, we've risen to the challenge. Why? Because we're women and we're awesome.

While I love that we embrace motherhood with wild abandon, we also know there is more to each of us. With the rise of social media and online businesses, it has become much easier to work from home. I am thankful for these opportunities. Some of my friends have online stores where they sell the fruit of their creativity. Some of my friends refinish furniture. Their talents are mind-boggling. Others have started photography businesses and sugar cookie businesses. Some of them write from home. Others make handmade signs that, unlike my dreams for hand-sewn dresses, people actually order. My cousin crochets adorable hats that look like animals. God has made each one of us unique as women.

And sometimes we cheer for each other, don't we? Sometimes, we feel so good about ourselves because we can see a tangible result of our efforts. It feels so good to hear we matter, to hear we're worth something.

But sometimes the cheers fall silent, the orders don't come in and the compliments fall short of the demand of our hearts.

As much as I believe we want to truly empower each other, at the same time, we are scared to death of each other. One woman's success somehow threatens ours. Why are her signs selling when mine aren't? Why does she have so many likes on her Facebook status and I have none?

Oh, we know this is wrong. We know we should be happy for each other. But it's hard. It's hard not to compare. It's hard not to place our worth on our performance. Maybe you work outside the home, and you are praised for your efforts. Or maybe you aren't even acknowledged, and it's eating away your confidence.

Let me tell you a little secret, precious mom. No type of performance, no matter how noble, valued, impressive, unvalued, unseen or unappreciated, gives us worth.

Not our success as moms.

Not our children's success.

Not our business or work success.

Not even one of them. Not even for a second. And not our failures, either.

Because, when we try to find our worth in any type of performance, we will always, no doubt about it, come up short. It will never be enough. The crowd will eventually get bored and find something or someone else to cheer about.

Remember that glorious race I told you about, where everyone cheered and saw me as the hero? The cheers that night were deafening. The cheers the next day were blaring. The cheers three days later were loud. A week later, faint. And within two weeks — silent.

The next year, a freshman sliced through my record. They hung her picture in the front office. And that night became a distant memory, one of which I'm probably the only person who even remembers.

If meeting your perfect standard of motherhood makes you feel better about yourself, then you have the same problem as me. If you feel worse about yourself when you don't meet your perfect standard of motherhood, then you have the same problem as me. There is no worth outside of who we are in Christ. No amount of success or failure will ever make us worth more or less than we already are.

This is easy to believe when we are talking about worldly success and failure. Most of us would probably agree that not becoming a millionaire doesn't affect our worth. We pat each other on the back when we don't get a promotion or job offer. We know that the silly world puts way too much emphasis on material possessions, and we spiritual people can't be bothered by the size of our houses or the extent of our closets. This is easy to believe.

It's much harder when we add the spiritual component.

When we fail at spiritual things, it becomes a different story. When our friends' kids wash each other's feet out of the goodness of their hearts and our kids can't even brush their teeth at the same time without hitting each other, it's harder to push away the voice that tells us we are nothing more than a disappointment.

Oh, how we long to be free of the comparisons and our own unmet expectations. But how? When it's right in our faces day in and day out, how do we measure up when we look at all the perfect people all around us and realize how incredibly not perfect we are?

There's a key found in the book of Psalms. Eugene Peterson puts it this way in *The Message*:

"No doubt about it! God is good, good to good people, good to the good-hearted. But I nearly missed it, missed seeing His goodness. I was looking the other way, looking up to the people."

God is good. Most of us would agree on this. It's us that are the problem, right? Well, sometimes, if we're honest, we're not all that sure about God, either. But we're sure about ourselves, right? No goodness here. *Look at how I reacted this morning!*

Let's put our goodness aside for a minute and go back to what we talked about in the last chapter about God and His never-ending, never-failing, wilder-than-we-can-imagine love.

When we are looking the other way, away from His love — *looking up to the people* — we will miss it. We'll miss this love freely poured out and available to us in every moment.

When we are so busy looking around at everyone else, we will miss the goodness of God. Not His goodness to humanity in general, but His goodness to us in our failures, in our shortcomings.

But wait a second ... doesn't this say He's good to good people? Doesn't that disqualify us?

Doesn't this mean that He's good to the moms who don't yell at their kids and wake up early to bake fresh blueberry muffins? Yes, He's good to them. They love their kids the same as the rest of us.

He's also good to the mom who just found out there isn't enough money in the bank to pay the mortgage, and the TV has been on all day to entertain her toddler while she tries to set aside her fear.

He's good to the mom who pressed the snooze button too many times, and everyone was late to school. He's good to the mom who promised herself she wouldn't yell today, and she only made it to 8 a.m.

He's good to the mom who made the valentines on Pinterest and feeds her kids organic food.

He's good to the mom who threw the frozen nuggets in the microwave because she worked until 6 and her son has a report due tomorrow.

Why? Because He's good to good people. And our goodness has nothing to do with our performance!

Goodness tied to performance of any kind is never sufficient. Worth tied to performance is always fleeting. Never good enough. Worth found in the goodness and love of God can silence the voice of failure in an instant.

You are not good because you are a good mom.

You are not good because you do good things.

You are good if you are a child of the King.

Look at these verses. I take that back. Don't just look — soak in these verses, until they seep out of you like syrup on Saturday morning pancakes.

"God made Him who had no sin to be sin for us, so that in Him we might become the righteousness of God." (2 Corinthians 5:21, NIV)

"Therefore, since we have been made right in God's sight by faith, we have peace with God because of what Jesus Christ our Lord has done for us. Because of our faith, Christ has brought us into this place of undeserved privilege where we now stand, and we confidently and joyfully look forward to sharing God's glory." (Romans 5:1-2, NLT)

"But the fruit of the spirit is love, joy, peace, patience, kindness, goodness, gentleness, faithfulness, self-control; against such things there is no law." (Galatians 5:22-23, ESV)

"Now He has reconciled you to Himself through the death of Christ in the physical body.
As a result, He has brought you into His own presence, and you are holy and blameless as you stand before Him without a single fault." (Colossians 1:22, NLT)

If you are in Christ, you are holy and blameless before Him.

But this is where it gets tricky.

This is where, while many of us know the truth, we struggle and strive to make ourselves look holy. Because even though we stare truth in the face, our experience tells us this simply cannot be true. The reflection in the mirror looks more like reality than the words in a book.

Here, in the dirt and grime of life, we know all too well that our hearts don't look very good. We're convinced that if God really saw what was in those hearts of ours, He'd surely withdraw His hand of goodness.

But, if we stop looking around at everyone else and look at Him, we would see something entirely different. He tells us in the book of Ezekiel:

> "Here's what I'm going to do ... I'll pour pure water over you and scrub you clean. I'll give you a new heart, put a new spirit in you. I'll remove the stone heart from your body and replace it with a heart that's God-willed, not self-willed. I'll put My Spirit in you and make it possible for you to do what I tell you and live by My commands." (Ezekiel 36:26, *The Message*)

This happens the moment you give your heart to Jesus. No striving. No performing.

> "This means that anyone who belongs to Christ has become a new person. The old life has gone; a new life has begun!" (2 Corinthians 5:17, NLT)

If you are in Christ, you are good. Psalm 73:1 applies to you. You have access to all the incredible goodness God can't wait to lavish upon you. In Him, you are made righteous. Your performance has nothing to do with it. And it's only when you look to Him and remember who you are in Him that you will be changed — changed into a mom who's free to love her kids because she's not striving for worth.

That's the beauty of this wild grace. But it takes time for our experience to catch up to reality. As long as you are looking the other way — up to the people — you will never believe it. You will miss experiencing God's goodness in your life because you will feel like you don't deserve it.

Yes, you will keep trying to find it. You will keep trying to earn it. And you will keep tripping on your own efforts.

Because you can't be good by trying harder. You can't be good by performing better.

Goodness comes from the grace of God. Undeserved. Unmerited. And irreversible.

You are worth so very much, sweet mama. You are worth the blood and life of Jesus, poured out on a cross so He could be with you. Right there in the mess of motherhood. Right there in your failures. Turn away from the crowd, and you'll hear something that will take your breath away.

Because once the crowd falls silent, you'll hear the sound of a Father, His heart beating fierce and fervent ... for you.

And oh, how He cheers!

Digging Deeper

1. Did you feel that you could measure your worth more easily before you became a mom?

2. In what areas do you try to find worth?

3. How much of your worth is tied to your performance? To your kids' performance? To your performance outside your home?

4. How often do you compare yourself and your success as a mom to other moms?

5. When do you feel the most worthless?

6. Do you feel like your goodness is tied to your performance?

7. In what ways have you been trying to "earn" goodness?

8. Have you missed God's goodness because you've been "looking up to the people"?

Chapter 4
The Things They Didn't Tell Us

It was a blistering Arizona June day. The kind of day when your mouth turns to cotton and the heat singes your lungs with every breath. The kind of day when you get out of the car and your butt sweat clings both to the seat and your shorts. Hello, clerk at the grocery store. No, I did not wet my pants. Yes, the air conditioning in my car works. My butt simply cannot breathe when it's 500 degrees. The walk from the car to the house leaves you delirious, and you are suffocating because the oven disguised as air has swallowed you whole.

On this lovely day, the sun beat down with a fervor, searing through skin like a laser through paper. They say it was one of the hottest days for June. They tell me about how they all nearly fainted in the chairs and in their suits. I don't remember, because I only cared about one thing that day. At the end of the aisle, laced with purple hydrangeas and white tulle, my prince stood waiting for me.

This was the day we had dreamed about. This was the day we thought would never come. As if time was standing still, or at best crawling its way around the calendar, June 15th could not arrive fast enough. This was the day when we would say our vows and bind our souls together as one.

We took premarital counseling, just like everyone suggested. We would walk out of the class laughing as they talked about the struggles we would face as husband and wife. Little did the experts know that we were different from all those people with all those problems.

We weren't going to fight about things like sex. Hello, didn't they know how long we had waited? We wouldn't have time to fight about finances because we'd be too busy with, well, you know. Did I mention we had waited a long time?

Communication? I love you, you love me. Let's get married, have three babies and do everything right that our parents did wrong. Seemed pretty simple to us.

Ryan and I met at Bible school in New Zealand. I do not lie when I say it could not have been a more romantic place to fall in love. Long talks by the river. Star-gazing in the meadow. Black sandy beaches on one side, white sandy beaches on the other and endless rolling green hills in between. You know the Shire in *Lord of the Rings*? I mean, the actual brilliant green hills where they filmed the Shire? We literally drove past it every Sunday on the way to church. White sheep and spotted cows sprinkled the landscape. Rugged cliffs and dangerous seas filled the horizon.

We hiked up waterfalls by jumping across boulders. We dove off cliffs into crystal-clear water. We sailed on little dinghies and traipsed through vast rainforests. We kayaked through caves covered in glow worms and watched the sun rise on the most eastern point in the world.

We laughed and cried and fell more deeply in love than I ever knew was possible. Within three weeks of dating, we knew it was meant to be. This man who stole my heart would hold it forever.

No one thought it would work. I lived in Arizona. He still had two years left of college in North Carolina. Long-distance relationships never work, they warned. We'd become one of those couples that simply drifts apart due to the distance. Little did they know just how much willpower this girl had. This is the girl who convinced her body she didn't need to pee. This is the girl who beat the high school record.

Beat the odds? Piece of cake.

One year after we returned from New Zealand, we stood before our friends, family and God and vowed the most sacred of vows.

But like most things in life — at least my life — nothing went as planned.

Everything about the wedding went wrong. My best friend's mom was going to sing. I grew up hearing her sing in church, and I always dreamed about her singing at my wedding. But in a twist of fate, she ended up in the hospital with a blood clot in her lungs. She was okay, and she still has a voice like an angel, but we had to find a replacement.

Ryan's aunt and uncle made the drive from Colorado. They walked Ryan through some significant times in his forming years, and they were going to read verses out of Song of Solomon. But on the way from Colorado, their son's appendix burst. He fought for his life for weeks, and praise God, he's still with us today. Ryan's aunt sat in the hospital, desperate for a miracle, while his uncle and other cousins left right after the ceremony. We found replacement Scripture readers.

If you haven't noticed by now, I tend to veer a bit toward the dramatic in my response to circumstances in life. I loved that man, though, and nothing was going to steal my joy.

Then the tuxedos for the groomsmen arrived crumpled at the bottom of a box. Why were they in a box, you ask? Well, my sweet groom knew someone in Florida who let us rent them for free. They arrived on my parents' doorstep two days before the wedding looking like they were stolen from a group of homeless men. When my well-meaning family told me we could steam out the wrinkles in the shower, I nearly lost my cool.

When you have sweat dripping down your back into your underwear, keeping your cool is no easy feat.

The wedding day arrived. Finally, regardless of all the problems we faced, my beloved and I would become man and wife. My mom and I showed up to the wedding venue late because my sister locked us out of the house on our way out the door.

To make an already chaotic situation worse, the wedding organizer lost all of our information. So my mom, instead of helping me get ready in the bridal suite, was outside trying to prevent a disaster.

I dreamed of my wedding from the time I was a little girl, so I had a pretty clear idea of what the day was supposed to look like. This day was nothing like the one I dreamed of.

I spent hours planning my bouquet with the florist. I wanted something bold. Something that was different from anything I had ever seen.

Boy, did I get it.

It was stunning. It truly was. The florist placed the long-stemmed lilies with splashes of lavender hyacinths like a baby cradled in my arms. There was a slight problem, however. The ribbon on my bouquet was still wet when she gave it to me for pictures, and when the last smile flashed for the camera, there was a lovely bright purple stain down the front of my dress.

Who brings white shoe polish with her from California to her friend's wedding? Thankfully, my friend.

I rode in on a horse-drawn carriage with my dad. The gasp from the crowd was exactly what I was anticipating, so that was one thing that went according to plan. All eyes on me, thank you very much. And yes, it's okay if I take your breath away.

Just as I arrived at the aisle, however, one of the ring bearers, my 2-year-old nephew, fell off the brick steps into the other ring bearer, my other 2-year-old nephew, and both of them toppled down the steps onto the unforgiving concrete. Needless to say, all eyes were no longer on me, and while their breath was momentarily taken, it wasn't because of my beauty. It was to see if my nephew would take a breath in between his cries. The screaming ring bearers were swiftly carried away, and the focus returned to yours truly.

The wedding itself was beautiful. My mom thought of everything, down to the smallest detail. Lights hung from trees. Flowers spilled from centerpieces. It could not have been lovelier. Friends and family stood beside us, vowing to help us through the ups and downs of marriage.

Sure, I thought. *How kind of you to offer.* But I was now standing beside my husband and happily-ever-after was waiting for us, so let's get this party started!

Except that the pastor, our principal from Bible school, pronounced us husband and wife using my maiden name and by the state of Texas instead of Arizona.

No biggie.

During the dancing, someone — let's be honest here, I know exactly who it was —stepped on my dress and ripped the bottom clean off. The servers drank all of the wine, and I left my passport in the bridal room. My dad brought it to the airport the next morning while the plane waited at the gate for us.

Oh, we won't have problems, we told those experts. We've got this marriage thing in the bag.

We wrote our own vows to each other. I vowed to submit, respect and honor him all the days of my life, no matter how bleak and hopeless it got. I vowed to follow him to the ends of the earth, and something about how we were so perfect for each other nothing could ever possibly stand in our way. He vowed to lead me, protect me, provide for me and always be everything to me forever and ever.

And then we grew up.

The experts, the opinion-givers, the invisible crowd of observers — "they" didn't tell us the struggles ahead would nearly tear us apart. They didn't tell us that we would deal with the ramifications of pornography for the majority of our marriage. They didn't tell us we would be asked to leave a stable job and all of our friends and march unprepared down to the jungle. They didn't tell us we would betray each other and hurt each other and hate each other.

They didn't tell us how hard it would be some days to choose to stay. To choose to love. To choose to fight. Some days, we stuck together out of sheer determination, and let's face it — pride. We wouldn't let the statistics win. We wouldn't let all the naysayers who thought we wouldn't make it have the last word.

They didn't tell us how risky love is, and that in giving your heart to another, you expose it to the harsh reality of a fallen world. Or maybe they did, and we just didn't listen.

They didn't tell us that having a baby would change things. Well, they probably did tell us that.

But they didn't tell us that postpartum depression would steal a year from our life.

They didn't tell us that poor choices would take years to earn back trust.

They didn't tell us that my fear would paralyze my adventurous spirit and cripple my joy.

They didn't tell us that we'd leave our fairy-tale and white-picket-fence dreams only to find ourselves lost in the wilderness of regret.

They didn't tell us that we'd be so exhausted from chasing kids, chasing the past and chasing happiness that we would lose each other in the madness.

We were in love. We were determined to get it right. What were those things they said we would fight about, again? We wouldn't have time for all of that, right?

I don't know where you are at in life right now. If you are reading this, then I am assuming you are a mother. Whether or not you carried your babies in your belly through pregnancy or in your heart through adoption, we are all mamas, and we love our kids.

But our stories are not the same.

You may have never had the chance to walk down that aisle, dreamy-eyed and fancy-free, because the one who stole your heart never showed up. You may have walked down into the loving arms of the man you thought would love you forever, but for whatever reason, those arms are no longer there. When affairs and addictions ravage your home, that wide-eyed dreamer you once were isn't the one you see in the mirror.

I don't know your story. I don't pretend to know what you are going through or what you have been through. But I've heard many of your stories. Whispers of betrayal. Tears of disappointment. Sobs of what should have been. I know your heart hurts. I don't know all the whys. But I know it's hard.

I've sat with friends whose husbands have found someone new. I've sat with women who feel worthless in the shadows of the sex-goddesses their husbands see on the internet. I hear the stories of pain and disappointment and despair.

I haven't just heard these stories. I've lived my own story.

How do you pick up the pieces of your shattered dreams? When the wounds are so raw and the heart so broken? When cancer shows its ugly face and declares its new plans for your life. When pornography steals your husband's desire for you. When sickness zaps your energy and questions riddle your mind. When a miscarriage swoops in and takes the life you longed to hold. When infertility makes conception work instead of art.

When your happily-ever-after becomes sadly-didn't-happen, being a good mom is one more card on the card stack. And it just might be the one that breaks the camel's back.

What do we do when life doesn't live up to our expectations? It's one thing when we don't live up to our own expectations. We can beat ourselves up and make promises that tomorrow will be different. But what about all the things that are out of our control?

Like husbands who don't turn out to be perfect.

And kids who don't do what we say.

And hearts that bleed for what could have been and what should have been.

They didn't tell us our stretch marks would make the mirror our enemy. They didn't tell us a child would rebel, despite all the prayers and well-meaning advice. They didn't tell us that some of our marriages would end, and we'd be left raising babies by ourselves. They didn't tell us it would be all we could do just to get out of bed some mornings.

They didn't tell us the whining would never stop.

They didn't tell us the trials would never end.

They didn't tell us it would be this hard.

But then again, maybe they did, and we just weren't listening.

When I look back on the little girl who walked down the aisle to that little boy, I am filled with both an unbelievable joy and an unshakable sadness. Because, when I look at those two all dressed up playing make-believe, I remember the girl I used to be. Wide-eyed and fancy-free, and so desperate for the approval of people. So desperate to be seen, to be loved, to be valued. And I want to hold her face in my hands and tell her it's going to be okay.

I want to tell her that the journey will be hard and unlike anything she expects, but it will be better than she can imagine.

I want to tell her that she doesn't have to spend a decade looking for worth in all the wrong places.

I want to tell her to let go of her white-knuckled grip on her dreams so she can see the joy to behold when she lives life with hands wide open.

I want to tell her that it's okay she didn't turn out to be perfect.

I want to tell her that it's okay her children didn't turn out to be perfect, too.

And if I could tell her then what I know now about God, maybe she could lay down her fear, her insecurities and her desperation right at His feet.

I wouldn't trade my story for anything. I can look back on my dreamy-eyed self, and although I would shield her from some of the heartbreak, I wouldn't choose a different path for her.

Ryan and I grew and fought and fell and clung. He loves me. But it's an imperfect, messy, flawed love. It couldn't satisfy my longings.

When he met my expectations of how a husband should love a wife, then I believed I could do anything — be anything. But when he failed — when he fell short of my hopes — insecurity showed its ugly fangs. When Ryan's love fell short of my insatiable hunger for worth, my insecurity, like a hungry dragon, demanded to be fed.

And it feasted on everyone around me.

Tell me I matter! Tell me you see me! Tell me that somehow, some way, I am enough.

And we all know what the whisper tells us in the dead of night — *never enough.*

White-picket-fence dreams coming true can't satisfy the deep longings of a broken heart. I thought that love would be enough. I was right — except for one thing. It wasn't my husband's love that could set me free. His love wasn't enough — isn't enough today. My dragon of insecurity is too hungry, and even the sacred love found in marriage isn't enough to fill the void.

I will never find fullness of life and power in a man, no matter how deep and marvelous our love grows. Because the truth is that life has a way of getting in the way.

But the love of God — the love that tells me I am enough because I am His — is enough to satisfy even the hungriest of hearts.

What do we do when life gets in the way of our dreams? When we walk with a limp today from the battle of yesterday? What dreams are you waiting for to come true? Does your happily-ever-after seem just out of reach, just around the corner? Will it come when your husband changes? When he gets that new job? When you buy the house of your dreams? When the next baby comes? When this stage of life is over? When the pain is gone and there's finally room for joy?

There's a woman in the Bible who knew well the tear-stained story of disappointment and betrayal. She knew well the angst of shattered dreams. You may have heard about her. She got the short end of the stick in many ways, and many of our stories look a lot like hers.

In the book of Genesis, chapter 16, we find a woman whose life got in the way of her happy ending.[1] Hagar was a servant, so she didn't get a say in most things in her life. Her purpose in life was to lay down her life for someone else.

God promised Abraham a son, but his wife Sarah got tired of waiting for the promise to come true. So she gave Hagar as a gift to Abraham. What a sweet wife. So considerate and selfless. They could have filmed a reality show on these people so shocking, the ratings would shatter through the ceiling.

Not surprisingly, Sarah started to get just a bit jealous of Hagar.

Hmmmm ... maybe giving my husband another woman to sleep with wasn't the best idea I've ever come up with.

But I'm sure you've heard this part of the story before. Hagar wasn't part of God's dream for Abraham and Sarah. They are the stars of this story, and

Hagar was the unfortunate sideshow — a speed bump on the way to the Promised Land.

And everyone sighs a breath of relief once she's gone.

Sarah's jealousy lashed out upon Hagar. She wanted her man back, and she was not thrilled with all the hanky-panky that had been going on.

So Hagar ran. Ran fast. Ran hard. Ran to nowhere. And she found herself in the vast wilderness of disillusionment and despair.

I don't know what Hagar was thinking, but I can imagine a few of the thoughts coursing through her mind.

They didn't tell me the joy wouldn't last.

They didn't tell me I would wake up alone.

They didn't tell me I was just a prop, just a means to an end.

They didn't tell me it was going to be this hard.

So here we find her, in the wilderness of what should have been but never was. As a little girl, surely she had dreams for her life. And surely, they didn't look like this.

But it's right here — in the sacred chasm between dreams and reality — where God met her. And He asked the question that gave her space to heal and freedom to dream again.

Hagar, where have you come from, and where are you going?[2]

He knew where she had come from. He knew her story. But He knew that she must remember before she could move forward. To know why she was wandering lost in the land of yearning unfulfilled, she had to go back to see where the train went off the tracks, where it all went wrong.

Where have you come from?

Sweet mama? Where have you come from? I picture you curled up on the couch, toes tucked under a soft blanket. I can see you waiting in the carpool line, preparing yourself for the hours ahead. I see you on your lunch break, wondering if you made the right choice to go back to work. I imagine you with a cup of coffee as you sit on your front porch while the kids play in the grass. Or stuck inside while snow locks you deep within the tomb of winter, nestled beside the fire while children run crazy on furniture. I envision you surrounded by mountains of laundry and mismatched socks. I picture you reeling with guilt from the patience lost and temper flared.

And God asks you the same question He asked Hagar in the wilderness that comes through the living of this life.

Where have you come from, sweet mama?

What disappointments have you faced? What wounds throb through your heart? What insecurities bind your courage? What betrayals follow you like a storm cloud, grumbling like thunder in your ear?

Where have you come from? What is your story?

Think long and hard. What did you expect this life to be like, and how short has it fallen from those expectations? What failures have led you to believe you're not enough and you don't have what it takes?

We must know where we have come from in order to get to where we are going.

And then He asks the next question.

Where are you going?

I know you go to the grocery store and the post office. You go to play dates and parks and Starbucks. You go to the gym and occasionally lock yourself in the bathroom, away from the maddening crowd. You might go to church and Bible study, and on the rare occasion, maybe out on a date.

But beyond the physical places that give our lives sanity, where are you going, sweet mama? Are you spinning crazy, trying to keep up with everyone else? Are you running from here to there, trying to gain the approval of people? Are you running to Facebook, Instagram and Pinterest to find yourself?

Jesus asked His disciples a similar question. After the crowds left because His teaching was too hard to understand, He looked at them and asked, "Do you, too, want to go?"

And Peter answered, "To where would we go? You alone have the words of eternal life."[2]

Where are you going, luv? To whom are you running? Where are you going to find worth? To find fulfillment? To find your happily-ever-after?

Your husband?

Your illusion that happiness is waiting just around the corner?

To the cheering crowd?

Or are you running backward, back into the hole of insecurity and fear?

Are you running back to what should have been, because it's better than what really is?

God asked Hagar these questions, then He listened as she told Him her pain, her sorrow, her disappointment. And He told her the greatest of news.

You're going to have a baby, sweet one.

Because we all know that babies make life easier, right?

But this baby is going to remind you of Me, Hagar. Every time you say his name, you will remember that I heard you. I heard your groans and your cries. My dreams for you are big, and they are going to come true. But now you need to get up and go live life.

And that's what Hagar did. She got up, and she went back to the living of this life. God promised that Ishmael, which means "God hears," would become a great nation. Hagar would have more descendants than she could count.

And she called God El Roi, "the God who sees," because He saw her there in the desert of broken dreams.[3]

You are seen, sweet mama. El Roi is close, whispering tender to your battered heart. He sees you in the piles of laundry. He sees you in the mess, in the chaos and in the frustration. He sees you when you fall and when you struggle. He sees you when the weight of betrayal overwhelms your heart. He sees you in your unmet expectations and secret longings. He sees you as you nurse your baby under the blanket of night. He sees you when you nurse your wounds, under the disguise of hope.

He sees you, and He asks. Where will you go, sweet one? Where will you take your pain, your dreams and your shattered hopes? Where will you take your guilt and your shame? To whom will you offer your barren womb, your empty arms or your hollow illusions?

Where are you going, sweet mama loved by God?

This isn't the end of Hagar's story. We find her yet again in the wilderness.[3] This time, her son is older, and it's his fault she's run away. He was bothering Isaac, the promised child. I wonder if she ever thought she could be a good mom if it weren't for her kid, too.

So Abraham strapped food and water on her shoulders and sent her on her merry way.

Let's remember that Hagar is Abraham's wife. This wasn't a one-night-stand, thanks-for-the-fun kind of arrangement. He married the girl. And now she was wandering once more in the land of thwarted longings. The water ran out. Ishmael was dying. Long gone were God's promises. Long forgotten was His tender presence. How much could one heart bear before it was crushed beneath the weight of sorrow?

The boy began to cry. And the tattered thread holding her battered mama heart together unraveled. And the pieces scattered across the desert floor.

Didn't God say her son would become a great nation? Had He forgotten His promises?

Had He forgotten her?

Have you ever asked that question? You've heard it before that God sees you. Maybe you've even experienced it firsthand. That moment when He reached into your brokenness and told you how precious you were to Him.

It's so easy to forget His promises when life sweeps our expectations right out from under our feet. When we're lying face down in the desert of what should have been but never will be, surrounded by the fragmented pieces of our hopes and dreams, we wonder where God is hiding.

All Hagar could see was her circumstance. And her circumstance looked pretty hopeless. She was a mom. She was all alone. She couldn't provide for her son, and if God did see her, then surely He just didn't care enough to act.

And God met her again in the desert of disillusionment.

Hagar, what's wrong?

What's wrong? I'll tell You what's wrong! This wasn't supposed to happen! I did what You said. I believed You and trusted You, and this is what I get? My son is dying. We're thirsty. And there is no water to be found.

And I can picture God, with His Daddy arms, scooping her up and holding her close. And He tells her the same thing He told her before: "Don't be afraid ... I will make a great nation from his descendants."[4]

Don't be afraid, Hagar. My promise still stands. I haven't changed. My promises haven't changed. Your circumstances, no matter how bleak, cannot change Me. I'm still the same. I'm still the God who sees you. Right here. Right now. The question is, how will your circumstances change you?

God's promises don't change based on our circumstances. The circumstances of life shape us. How they shape us — who we become because of them — is always our choice. It's in the seeing, in the remembering, that we lean into love and are then transformed into love.

"Then God opened Hagar's eyes, and she saw a well full of water. She quickly filled her water container and gave the boy a drink."[5]

Sweet mama, the well was already there. It was there all along. Right there waiting for her. Hope stood guard around Hagar, but she just couldn't see it through the ache. The God who sees her opened her eyes so she could see Him and His wild love for her. She couldn't see the well because her circumstances blinded her. She was so focused on what should have been that she couldn't see what actually was — that she was lavishly and irrevocably adored by a God who sees every tear, every disappointment, every betrayal and every unfulfilled dream. She drank deep from the well, and I'm certain she forevermore saw life through a different lens.

You are loved by the God who sees you. His promises to you stand firm regardless of how dry and deserted the wasteland of your life might seem.

The question is, what do you see?

Right now, in your circumstances, what are you choosing to see? Is your eyesight blurry from too many shed tears to count? Is it out of focus because you've been listening to too many voices and you're worried about too many opinions? Are you blinded by your circumstances and splintered longings? Has life got so far in the way of your expectations that you can only look back and wonder where it all went wrong?

The well is right in front of you, sweet one. It's Him. He's here. He's got you in His Daddy arms, and He shouts love when He whispers your name.

They didn't tell me that marriage would expose the unhealed wounds of my brokenness.

They didn't tell me that motherhood would unmask the insatiable appetite of my insecurities.

They didn't tell me I'd be so lonely, afraid and empty.

They didn't tell me it would be this hard. And I wouldn't have listened even if they had.

But does it really matter what they did or didn't tell us? Their voices aren't the ones that matter, and it's time to stop listening to "them," anyway. One voice tells me that He loves me. One voice tells me that He sees me. And the day that I believe that's enough is the day I will realize I'm already exactly where I wanted to be all along — in Him, drinking from the well that mends my broken heart back together.

He sees you, mama. He hears you, mama. He knows life didn't turn out the way you thought it would. He sees you in the wilderness of endless dirty diapers, temper tantrums, snotty noses and bad attitudes. He sees you as you chauffer kids from activity to activity. He sees you as you teach in your home and cook at your stove. He sees you as you rock a baby who can't be soothed. He sees you as you fix dinners that no one wants to eat. He sees you as you show up every day without cheers and without affirmation. He sees you, and He tells you one thing:

Do not be afraid.

This is the paradox of life. When grace draws near and cloaks the weary with the blanket of love. When we let ourselves rest in the warmth of love's embrace, we find that it's the shattered dreams that actually lead us to grace.

It's the broken promises that lead us to truth. And when we're wrapped up in the cocoon of both grace and truth, we're transformed into women who have known the wild love found only in the wilderness. When we remember where we have come from and realize there's only one place we want to go, the fairy-tale ending of happily-ever-after loses its appeal. We are drawn again and again to the One voice that tells us all we ever really needed to know. And we can see ourselves the way He sees us.

As *loved*.

And all the broken pieces of life, of hearts and dreams and disappoint-ments, seam together as the thread of grace weaves in and out of the pain, the sorrow, the joy and the laughter. Together, joy and grief in the hands of grace mold the woman you are becoming until a tapestry of crazy grace becomes your story.

And your story — this tapestry of grace — becomes the mantel extending from your life, wrapping tightly around the weary souls around you. For we are all thirsty for the well.

Receive grace, dear one. And then offer a cold cup to another thirsty mama.

Digging Deeper

1. What were your fairy-tale dreams for your life that haven't turned out how you expected?

2. How has motherhood brought out the dragon of insecurity in you?

3. Where have you come from? What betrayals and disappointments have brought you into the wilderness?

4. Where are you going? To whom and to where are you running with your insecurities and disappointments right now?

5. What are you choosing to see right now in your circumstances? In your kids? In your marriage? In your relationships? What is blinding you from hope right now?

Chapter 5

Treasures in the Darkness

"When will they be ready?" he asks for the tenth time today.

"I don't know, little man. Soon, though."

"What will they look like?"

"I'm not sure. But I bet they'll be beautiful."

He watches, waiting for the moment when the butterflies burst forth from their tombs, afraid if he peels his eyes away for even an instant, he'll miss it.

He's been watching for two weeks now. They came as larvae. I watched them grow into caterpillars. He watched them inch to the top, spin their webs and create their shells of transformation. Now he watches their stillness, wondering what could possibly be taking so long.

For a 5-year-old, two weeks is an eternity.

As he watches, he doesn't realize that I'm watching him. Watching in awe as he grows and changes. Watching in pride as he spins and creates. Waiting in anticipation for the moment his eyes are opened to the truth, the moment he bursts forth from the tomb and into salvation, a new creation. I could push him. I could convince him. If I asked him if he wanted Jesus to enter into his tiny heart, he would say yes. But I want it to be because he's seen Jesus with his own little eyes. I want my son to accept Jesus because he sees those nail-scarred hands and can't help but fall into their safety. It will happen. Soon. The time is close. He's almost ready.

In the meantime, I watch. I wait.

For a mother, five years is but a moment.

And as I watch, I feel the eyes of Someone watching me. Watching in awe as I grow and change. Watching in pride as I discover and create. Waiting in anticipation for the moment when I burst forth from the tomb of my insecurity and performance-driven worth and into the fullness of freedom in truth. He could push me, but He doesn't. Instead, He carries me once again with those nail-scarred hands. His eyes watch, but they don't wonder. They know. They already see who I will be. Those eyes are the same eyes that formed me in the dark. Those eyes have seen every plummet, every tear, every dream. And those eyes see not only where I have been, but who I will become.

For a King, a lifetime is only the beginning.

A little boy watches as caterpillars become butterflies. A mother watches as her little boy becomes a man. And a King watches as a woman becomes His bride.

Here in this sacred cocoon of motherhood, we are transformed. But transformation always happens in the dark. A butterfly transformed inside its cocoon. A seed reborn within the soil. A diamond hewn beneath the mantle of the earth. A mother molded within the lonely walls of her home. Yes, transformation always happens in the dark. And darkness is the loneliest place on the planet.

I want to tell you that I'm strong. I want to tell you that I have it all together. When you watch my life, I want you to think that I am an incredible mom, wife and friend. I want you to see how completely confident I am in my worth in Christ. After all, why would you think a crazy lady stuck in a pit of depression has anything to say? There's always the temptation to pretend to be someone I'm not. And I realize that I fool no one with this charade.

I will be honest with you. I thought that being a mom would be the most wonderful thing I would ever experience. While I love my children desperately, and I have experienced more joy in loving them than I ever knew was possible, my journey as a mom has been dark.

Dark. Lonely. Scary.

At times, my soul feels enveloped in darkness. No matter how hard I try, I can't perform well enough. My efforts aren't good enough. I never live up to my promises to be a better mom. I look around and see all the other moms who are getting it right. I see their efforts, and I try to match them. But I fail. I can't keep up. I'm not strong enough, wise enough or patient enough. Why keep chasing the illusion of victory? Is it better to just bow out of the fight? Hand over the trophy to the enemy?

Have you ever felt this way?

For years, I cried, "What do I need to do, God? What do You want me to do?"

Nothing but darkness echoed in reply.

After returning to the States from Costa Rica, we spent a year in North Carolina attempting to regain our footing. While I grappled with postpartum depression, both Ryan and I struggled with our self-proclaimed status as missionary failures. Ryan comes from a long line of life-long missionaries. We were the first to come home sooner than planned. As a child, I dreamed of running an orphanage. Yes, in addition to my own little flock, I was to be the rescuer of all those other little hearts, too. But there we were, back from the field, wounded warriors limping home with our heads hung low.

A ministry internship opened up in Colorado. It seemed like the perfect solution for our battered hearts. We had to raise support, though, and in 2008, as the economy spiraled down the drain, people held tightly to their funds. We spent the next two years praying for a miracle that never came as every employment door slammed shut in our faces. In the meantime, our precious little Emery arrived. So there we were, dependent on food stamps, three kids under the age of 4 and a mama looking for hope in all the wrong places.

Ryan eventually found a job, and we began the one-foot-in-front-of-the-other path to healing. Unfortunately, I thought healing meant doing. And so I did a lot. A whole lot. It was during these years that God began rousing a dream within me to speak and write. I marveled at the opportunities He provided, and I am forever grateful to a few precious women who breathed wisdom into the vision growing within my heart. I began teaching and writing, hungry for applause and desperate for hope. God somehow used my feeble attempts and built a ministry out of nothing.

As our family grew and our values shifted, we decided it was time to leave our church, which meant leaving my ministry. Like ripping a bandage that's been left on the skin too long, leaving my ministry bared open the rawness of my self-doubt I kept hidden behind my theology and knowledge. The ministry that told me I was worth something was now gone, and the walls of my home closed in tighter around my heart.

A close friendship ended during this time. The betrayal awakened my dragon of insecurity yet again, and so began its feeding frenzy on my confidence. Our extended family walked through several life-altering events, and the thread holding our marriage together slowly unraveled as sin (both his and mine) pulled us down even further into the pit where shattered dreams reside.

My misconceived ideas of God and worth and life fueled my insecurity, like frenzied wind on seething embers, and my self-doubt kindled into self-loathing. No matter how hard I tried, I failed at every turn. I couldn't become the mom, the wife and the woman I thought I should be. No matter how many promises I made, my efforts felt like bailing water from a sinking ship. Whispers in my ear convinced me that God was not only disappointed in me, but that He had turned His back on me. This awareness jolted me, waking me up to what I had known all along. Staring face to face with reality, I could only come to one conclusion:

I was unworthy of love. Unworthy of friendship. Unworthy of anything good from God.

Everything I had built my worth upon crashed down like that house built upon the sand. The storms came, and down it fell. We pulled away from church, tired of the politics and run-around involved with ministry. I was burned out on religion, and I grew disillusioned with God. He wasn't answering my prayers, and I grew tired of waiting for miracles that never came.

In my isolation, I turned my efforts once again to my children, desperate to become everything they deserved.

I found out quickly that they were not very good cheerleaders.

But I kept trying. I kept striving. I read books and blogs, waking up each morning with renewed determination to get it right. I read one particular book that said if I really loved my kids, I would homeschool them. I didn't want to homeschool my kids, but this book convinced me that they would be ruined if I didn't, and fear — my constant companion — gripped tightly around my heart. I'm sure the author meant well. But like I said before, I love my kids. Wouldn't I do anything to give them the best chance possible in this life? And so I did what the book told me to do and began homeschooling.

Homeschooling is a beautiful thing, and I am astounded by my precious friends who wake up in the morning excited to spend the whole day with their kids. I am not one of those moms. I've mentioned that I love my kids to pieces, right? Well, my love has trouble expressing itself when we get to the umpteenth hour of the day. God has given some of you an extra dose of strength that He didn't give to me. Yet, in the emptiness of the applause, I felt compelled to pull my children out of school in an effort to achieve my status as supermom.

You heard what happened when we tried baking cookies. Need I say more about what our days looked like now?

Please hear me when I say that I love my homeschooling friends. What you are doing is noble and brave. But only if you are doing it for the right reasons. I, however, was doing it for all the wrong reasons, and I found myself sinking quickly in the sands of utter and total failure.

At the same time, my marriage began unraveling before my eyes. Bitterness etched its mark across our story, and loneliness became my closest friend. Ryan traveled for work four days a week, winter dragged itself all the way into summer and each new day loomed like a tsunami over the horizon.

A darkness unlike anything I had known before shrouded my days. I didn't know which way was up, and all I could think about was which way was out. *Where's the exit door, because this is too much for me.* Another failure. How did all the other moms do it? They came to our support group bubbling over with excitement at the next project.

I dreaded waking up each day.

My closet became my haven. I tried clawing my way back to God. Cloaked in loneliness and convinced of worthlessness, tears painted my cheeks and questions riddled my mind.

What do You want me to do, God? What is wrong with me? Why can't I just get my act together and figure this thing out? I thought I was strong, but I don't even recognize myself anymore.

And in the darkness of that closet, I heard God whisper to my heart.

Melissa, who are you?

I didn't know how to respond. *What? What do You mean? I'm a mom, a wife ... a mess. That's who I am.*

And then came the question that changed my life.

Who are you without all that? Now that everything else is stripped away, who are you? Without your kids, your ministry, your applause ... or your failures. Who are you?

I responded with the only answer I could dredge up through the chaos spinning in my mind.

I have no idea.

And that beautiful voice of the One who calls me out of darkness and into His glorious light spoke deep in my soul.

Good. Now let Me tell you who you are. Everything else is a façade. They might cheer for you. They might ignore you. But I know who you really are. Let Me show you.

And so began my journey out of my dark chrysalis.

The thing about darkness is that it comes upon you unexpectedly. When afternoon surrenders to twilight, our eyes adjust as the darkness encroaches around us. We don't realize it's even dark until we can't see anything. Even then, our eyes find a way to adjust.

Such a remarkable creation, this body we live in, isn't it?

Just as evening glides ever so gently into night, the stars making their appearance one by one, the enemy doesn't knock on the door and demand for us to hand everything over to him. No, he's much more cunning than that. He steals things bit by bit.

Slowly. Stealthily. Until suddenly we wonder where our joy has gone.

What happened to the mom who saw big dreams for her family? What happened to the marriage that wouldn't succumb to the ranks of statistics? Where is the heart that refused to give in to the status quo?

If we think back, we won't remember when we gave it away. It happened right before our eyes, but when we weren't looking.

As darkness circles, our hearts adjust, and hopelessness becomes the norm. Insecurity rules the day, and worthlessness follows close behind.

Moses knew darkness. When the people built a golden calf and God refused to go any farther with them on their way to the Promised Land, Moses begged God to change His mind. He knew that without God's presence, any attempt was futile. So God listened. And to prove it, He told Moses, "I will make all My goodness pass before you" (Exodus 33:19). Doesn't that sound lovely? God's goodness passing by. Isn't that what we all long for?

Give us Your goodness, God!

But here's the catch. For Moses, and for us, it required darkness first.

In verses 21-22, the Lord continued, "Look, stand near Me on this rock. As My glorious presence passes by, I will hide you in the crevice of the rock and cover you with My hand until I have passed by."

It must have been dark hidden there under God's hand.

There, under God's hand. The hand that formed Adam out of the dust and Eve out of the rib hovered over Moses. The hand that holds this world covered Moses there in the crevice of a rock. I wonder if Moses resisted. I wonder if he tried to push it back, scared that God didn't know what He was doing.

Isn't that what we do? Resist the pain. Push against the trials. Scared to death that God doesn't know what He's doing, and if He does, then He certainly can't be trusted.

Can God's goodness really be in the pain? Is His presence really found in the dark? Could it be that the darkness is actually the safest place we could be? Could it be that when we feel life can't get any darker, it's because we are secured in the crevice of the rock, hidden by a nail-scarred hand while God's goodness passes by? And if we stopped wrestling that hand, maybe, just maybe, we would catch a glimpse of His glory?

Could it be that in the lonely, dark valleys of motherhood, this is the place where we might see God's goodness passing by?

Isaiah 43:5 says, "I will give you treasures hidden in the darkness — secret riches. I will do this so you will know that I am the Lord, the God of Israel, the One who calls you by name" (NLT).

This verse crumbles my small view of God where He grants all my desires and shields me from all the pain in this life. I want the glory, the esteem, the applause. That doesn't happen very often in life. Reality blows in and sweeps my dreams out from under me. The mom who wanted to gather her chicks close flew the coop again and can't seem to find her way back.

But the riches found in the darkness are worth more than any prize found in the applause of this world.

Take a look at the butterfly. Hidden within the darkness of its cocoon, transformation takes its slow, painful course. And then it pushes out, its wings bursting with the newness of a life that could only come from its time in the dark. It can never be the same again. Its days of inching across leaves are over. It was created to fly. It was made to soar.

So were you and I.

We'll never see the clouds if we stay there on the ground. Apart from little boys, no one gasps in awe at a caterpillar. A butterfly, though. It can float in from anywhere, and everyone nearby jumps up to look. They point to others.

"Did you see it? Look over there!"

You and I are image bearers of God. When we soar, people catch a glimpse of God. And His goodness passes by.

We run from darkness, though, don't we? Isn't it interesting that children are afraid of the dark? What is it about the dark that floods them with fear? It's there in the dark where monsters and boogey men hide. Darkness breeds fear, doesn't it?

I have a reoccurring dream where I enter my house in the black of night and none of the lights work. I'm frantic to find a light switch that works, but to no avail. There is nothing coming after me that I can see. There's no danger to be found. But my heart races, desperate to escape the darkness. Desperate for the security of the light.

But transformation almost always happens in the dark, and when we lay down our preconceived ideas of who God is and what He should do for us, we can rest in the crevice of the rock, safe under His hand.

What crevice do you find yourself in right now? What darkness are you facing that has you lonely, lost and afraid? In what areas of life are you crying out, *God, where are You? And where is Your goodness for me?*

Do you remember Lazarus in the darkness of his tomb?[1] Bound in his grave clothes, he lay alone in the vault of night. Until he heard Jesus call him by name. And then everything was different.

He couldn't go back to who he used to be. His illusions of who God was and what he should do for Him remained behind. He now knew the voice of his Jesus, and no other voice in the world mattered any longer.

In the darkness of the tomb, God's transforming power is at work, gently changing us into who we are meant to be — into who we already are but just don't know yet.

But first we must die. Die to our preconceived ideas of who we think God should be. Die to both our self-righteousness and our self-hatred. Die to the notion that we have to perform in order to be of worth. And then we stand, called out of the tomb by the voice of Jesus, standing fully alive and fully awake to both God's presence and our worth.

When we stop running from the darkness and instead get on our knees and start looking for the treasure, we'll find He was there all along. He wants to be found. And then suddenly we'll realize that it's actually in the darkness that we see HIM. We'll realize that it is in the tombs of life where we find the revelation of His heart.

The failure you can't get over is actually the greatest expression of His grace.

The person who hurt you is actually the stairway to a new level of His affection.

The loss of one dream is actually the doorway to a place greater than your wildest dreams.

It is true that God calls us out of darkness and into His glorious light, but the treasures found in the darkness open our eyes to what we couldn't see before.[2] No, you weren't created to live in darkness. But what if we stopped shaking our fists at God because of the darkness and instead started seeking the treasure found in the darkness? As Stephen Smith writes in *The Lazarus Life*, "The truth is, you do not belong in the tomb. Every tomb of life is too small for you. It is the brief interlude before the abundant life you were meant to live, before the reality of transformation, before the moment you hear Jesus speaking into the darkness."[3]

He's speaking, sweet mama. He's calling your name. Are you listening?

During my time in the tomb, I kept asking God, *What do You want me to do?* Because healing means doing, right? If I am not doing something to make myself better, then how will I ever find healing? If I'm not working on myself, feeling bad about myself, how will I do better tomorrow? Isn't conviction good? Doesn't God want me to be a good mom? How will I find healing from my anger, my bitterness, my impatience unless I DO SOMETHING ABOUT IT?!

That's what I heard on Sundays.

That's what I read in the books and articles and posts.

Try this, do that — and of course, why aren't you doing that?

The answer came to me in that dark closet. My Abba scooped me up, laid me against His chest and said, *You don't have to do a thing, sweet one. In fact, all your doing and trying is only making things worse. Let's try things My way for a bit.*

But how, God? Tell me. I'll do anything. What do You want me to do?

He squeezed me just a little bit tighter, my ear pressed up against His heart.

Be still and know that I AM GOD.[4]

So I sat awhile and then tried to jump back down and try again. Isn't that what our days look like so often? Read a snippet of the Bible and then jump down to try again. Find some conviction in a sermon and run out the door ready to do things differently. Pray a quick prayer for God's help through the day, then dash out the door ready to take on the world. Only to crawl back through the door, head hanging in shame.

A quiet time isn't enough. It isn't about getting a little of Jesus on Sunday or in the morning and then hoping that's enough to get you through. It's not about spending hours on your knees in prayer. It actually has nothing to do with time at all. It is a moment by moment, clinging to the Vine, abiding in His presence in every second of every day.[5]

When I tried to jump back down and run along my merry little way, Abba's arms scooped me up yet again. And again He whispered, strong arms holding me tight.

Stay a bit longer. In fact, how about you never leave at all? Stay here all day, up against My heart. Live life from this vantage point. Love your children from this view. Love your husband from here. And watch what I can do when you stop trying.

Staying still is much harder than trying hard.

But don't You want me to be a good mom, God? Don't You want me to be a good person?

And that Daddy of mine, who never once loosened His grip on me, spoke light into my night.

I want to know you're loved. When you live loved, you'll live free.

And that's when I realized that the longer I stay with my ear pressed against His heart, my heart slows and catches the rhythm. The longer I listen, the more I grow used to the beat and begin to live in accord with it. Not dancing to my own beat, not beating my own drum of self-righteousness or my head in self-loathing. Simply dancing in tune with the heart that beats with songs of rejoicing over me.

Can we ever truly KNOW God unless we are still? Unless we stop wrestling against His hand? Can we ever truly know ourselves until we stop striving and spinning and measuring? Can we ever hear the One who calls us by name if we're too busy listening for the roar of the crowd?

I'm not a fan of New Year's resolutions. I'm more of the daily resolution kind of girl.

Today, I won't yell at my kids.

Today, I won't get mad when my husband comes home late.

Today, I will let go of that hurt.

Today, I won't eat 10 chocolate chip cookies.

Today, I will be patient, kind, loving, skinny, energetic — perfect.

You can see how far my resolutions have brought me. It's a recipe for disaster. It's a recipe for darkness.

For six months, I did nothing but listen to the beat of my Abba's heart. Moment by moment, I listened.

When my anger got the best of me, I listened.

When I felt afraid, I listened.

When I felt less than, I listened.

When the loneliness threatened to take me under, I listened.

When I felt overwhelmed, I listened.

When my kids misbehaved, I listened.

When the house was a mess, I listened.

When I thought my heart could bear no more, I listened.

I stopped trying to be a better mom.

I stopped trying to control my anger. I stopped trying to be patient. I stopped trying to be healed. I stopped trying to change myself.

I flew the coop of my own perfection and began resting in God's perfection.

And do you want to know what happened? I looked back on who I was six months before, and I couldn't even recognize that girl anymore.

I didn't yell at my kids as much. I didn't dwell on the past as much. I didn't feel like a failure anymore. I laughed more and judged less.

I also put my kids back in school and forgave myself in the process.

What do You want me to DO, God???

Nothing.

Don't you see, sweet mama? We don't have to do anything to be worth something. All our efforts, our performance and success — they won't satisfy the cravings deep within. They won't fill the hollow space in our hearts only Jesus can fill.

Our kids can't fill this space, either. Their accomplishments and success don't make you a better mom. The only way to be a better mom is to sit still long enough against the heart of Jesus until you believe you are really who He says you are. You are worth more than you could possibly know, but you must turn off the noise of the crowd in order to hear it.

I have an idea. Let's make a new resolution today. Let's let go of our strivings for worth. Let's let go of our need to perform and compare. Let's let go of making our kids the best at everything. Today, let's be still and know HE IS GOD.

Today …

Instead of trying to be a good mom, I will be still and know that HE IS GOD.

Instead of trying to be patient, I will be still and know that HE IS GOD.

Instead of trying to overcome my anger, I will be still and know HE IS GOD.

Instead of trying to measure up to who I think I should be, I will be still and know HE IS GOD.

Instead of trying to manipulate my dreams into reality, I will be still and know HE IS GOD.

Instead of trying to find purpose, I will be still and know HE IS GOD.

Instead of trying to muster up grace for others, I will be still and know HE IS GOD.

Instead of striving for worth, I will be still and know HE IS GOD.

It's in the dark that we find the hidden riches of God's presence. Once we realize that even on our best day our efforts aren't enough, and we stop pushing against God's hand, we will find the riches found in the darkness. Riches of far more value than the fleeting applause of the crowd.

The disciple John called himself the disciple Jesus loved.[6] This claim seems arrogant at first glance. Jesus loves everyone, right? How dare one person claim to be the ONE Jesus loves? How could John have such confidence in this truth?

We catch a glimpse of his relationship with Jesus in the Upper Room during the Last Supper. In the book of John, we find John leaning against Jesus' chest. So close, he can hear His heart beating.

This is the same John who, weeks before, was asking Jesus to give him a place of honor in the coming Kingdom.[7] John wanted to make sure his worth was secure. He wanted to know just where he stood in comparison with everyone else. Can you hear what he's really saying?

Tell me that I matter! Tell me that I'm worth something!

Sound familiar?

There in the Upper Room, though, his cries fall silent. He was just still. He was just listening. Darkness loomed. Despair waited just around the corner. Yet, here in the stillness, he listened. He listened to the heartbeat of Jesus.

And what he would see in the coming hours would show him the cry of his Abba's heart.

The coming hours, when darkness hung so heavy the sun could not bear its weight, the heart of Jesus beat with love so deep, it conquered the darkness. It beat so outlandishly with love, it conquered John's doubts. John heard the same heart beating that would drip blood and die for a world lost in darkness. Once John heard his Abba's heart beating for him, he didn't need the place of honor anymore. He was safe knowing he was loved. And that love allowed him to live with a boldness unlike anything he could have ever dreamed up on his own.[8]

The heart of Jesus beats still today. His heart beats with a never-ceasing, never-failing love for you and for me, too. But we must be still long enough to hear it. As the darkness looms, as our failures crouch, as the cheers of the crowd fade into the night, the heart of Jesus beats with the steady rhythm of the deepest love.

And you don't have to do a single thing.

Oh, precious mama, will you let your Father speak to your heart today? Will you allow His sweet voice to sing over you as you fold the laundry, wash the dishes, change dirty diapers and break up fights? The shadows of fear, depression, hopelessness, anger, anxiety and loneliness will run as Jesus absorbs the mess.

He came to invade our darkness. He came to invade our hopelessness. He came to invade our plans, our dreams and our days. He came to invade our hearts. And maybe if we're still long enough, we will actually KNOW Him. Not the God we've conjured up in our heads. Not the God we think He should be. Not the God we expect to find. No, we will KNOW Him as HE IS.

Guess what happens next? He'll show you who YOU REALLY ARE. Not the mom you think you should be. Not the person you've conjured up in your mind. Not the person your parents wanted you to be, or the wife your husband thinks you should be. Not the best cook, teacher, lawyer, doctor, writer, director or mom. But you, stripped from all of the fluff, all of the pretense.

And let me tell you, YOU, the REAL YOU, take your Father's breath away.

He's watching you in the sacred cocoon of motherhood. This dark, lonely place. Watching and waiting for the moment you burst forth as the woman He already knows that you are. And this is only the beginning. He's still shaping you, like a potter at his wheel. But He's the One doing the shaping. He's the One working out the transformation there in your cocoon.

You need only to be still.

It's in the darkness where God woos us to Himself, sweet mama. There, in the crevice of the rock, we're hidden safe beneath His hand. When we stop pushing against Him, letting go of our failures and unmet expectations of life, we'll discover the treasures waiting for us right there in His shadow. And maybe, just maybe, the world lost in the darkness, searching ever for the light, will look our way and realize that the girls with great Facebook posts aren't there anymore.

No, they will look our way and stop for just a moment because they see God's goodness passing by.

***There are times when medication is necessary to treat depression. This is in no way an attempt to tell you to stop taking medication or feel guilty if you need it. God can use modern medicine to bring healing. If this is you, please know that my heart is for you. Even as you take your medication, be still and hear your Father's heartbeat. He speaks love over you, sweet one!

Digging Deeper

1. Has your journey as a mom ever felt dark and lonely to you?

2. How has God revealed treasures to you in the darkness?

3. How are you resisting the darkness — pushing against His hand?

4. In what ways are you trying to become a better mom or person?

5. Are you too busy listening to the voice of the crowd or the voices of insecurity to hear the whisper of God to your heart right now?

6. What would it look like to simply be still and rest against the heartbeat of Jesus?

7. What scares you about being still? What feelings of guilt are you clinging to?

8. How is God's goodness passing by in your life right now?

Chapter 6
It's Not Barbie's Fault

The afternoon sun beats mercilessly against the paper-thin windowpane. Its intensity threatens to crack the glass. Sweat beads across my forehead. The air is heavy with moisture, and my heart is heavy with worry. The pink flowers flecked across the pale green walls of the nursery mock me as I remember the hours I sat dreaming before my daughter arrived.

In the early mornings, as the earth erupts with song, I sat staring at these walls, caressing my swollen belly, imagining the joy and delight I would soon know beyond the walls of my imagination. I sat in this same rocking chair, its creaking melody singing promises of motherhood over me, as I waited for labor to begin.

Now the creak of the rocking chair can't be heard above the deafening screams spewing from the very real bundle in my arms. My heart races as I attempt to calm her. Her downy skin is flushed with both the southern summer heat and her fierce, determined spirit. Her face is pinched with anger, blood rushing to her cheeks in passion. Her screams pierce both my ears and my heart as exhaustion overwhelms me.

What am I doing wrong? Why won't she nurse? The doctor said she should nurse for 45 minutes, and it's only been five. Maybe she needs a bottle? Maybe my milk isn't enough for her.

No, my milk has to be enough for her. I have to be enough for her. This is what I was born to do.

I press her back to my chest, convincing myself that if I keep trying, I will succeed. Despite the pain from cracked and bleeding nipples — which, by the way, "they" didn't tell me about, either — I am determined to feed her from the wellspring of my body. She doesn't want the wellspring of my body, though. More screaming. She squirms, tiny arms and legs matching my determination.

With a sigh of defeat, I rise up out of the chair and head to the kitchen. With a howling baby in one arm, I measure and pour formula in the bottle with the other. I couldn't pump enough milk to fill a bottle, so with another pang of guilt, I heat up the bottle.

Poison. That's what they said this was.

I swallow my guilt and place the bottle in her mouth. She turns her head, uninterested in what I have to offer. Milk spews across her face, trickles down my skin and forms a pool in the crook of my arm. I rock her. I bounce her. I sing lullabies. I pray prayers. Nothing calms her down. Nothing I do makes any difference.

Panic, like bile, rises from the pit of my stomach.

I can't take this anymore. I'm doing everything they said to do.

What's wrong with her? What's wrong with me?

Voices of friends scatter across the corridor of my mind. They said it would be beautiful — that I would love every second. Thoughts of insecurity tumble out of doors I've tried to lock, but the screaming leaves me weak, and I let them loose. Their taunting reminds me of all the ways I'm not enough. All the ways I don't measure up.

Words from books I've read leap off the pages and drip like venom into my mind. The advice of well-meaning friends and family members echoes beyond the screaming. And as all the words collide into each other, they form themselves into one giant word that screams louder than my infant's cries.

One word that would ensnare me within a tangled, unyielding web of shame.

FAILURE.

It's all around us. On our computers, at our kids' schools, in our churches and Bible studies, in our playgroups and — more than anything — in our minds.

No one is saying it to us directly. No one looks into our eyes and says, "Wow, you are one big, fat, stinking failure."

But we feel it. We feel it when they say, "Oh, you only nursed for four months? They say you should nurse for two years so your baby can get full brain development."

Is that why my kids can't follow directions? Is that why they forget everything I say the second after I say it?

Is that why they act surprised every morning when I ask them if they've brushed their teeth, as if it's some new fad all the moms are trying? Is it because their brains aren't actually fully developed inside those heads?

I'm sorry, you sweet children of mine. I tried. You didn't want full brain development. Really, it's your fault. I stuffed my nipple in your mouth while you bawled and gagged, and you chose to have an underdeveloped brain. So sorry about that.

We feel it when they say, "Is that your son at the top of the play structure? He could really get hurt. The other kids might want to try it, too. He should probably come down, don't you think?"

Climbing happens to be something my boy did — a lot. Not all boys have an innate desire to see how many heart attacks they can give their mother in the span of a few short years, but mine did.

Maybe it goes back to the brain development thing.

I tried to make him play quietly on the ground, but he ate the mulch. I tried to let him swing on the swings, but he climbed out. I encouraged him to play tag. He tackled the girls, and they all cried.

We started going to the park during non-visiting hours.

I hear it when they say their kids are best friends and mine can't sit in the back seat of the car together without trying to strangle each other.

I hear it when they tell me, "Boy, you sure have your hands full!"

No one has ever offered a helping hand after making that comment. I guess they thought the reminder was somehow helpful. Helpful in making me feel like crap, that's for sure.

I hear it when a friend announces she fits back into her pre-pregnancy jeans after only six weeks.

I hear it when I remember dropping off my pre-pregnancy jeans at Goodwill almost a decade ago.

I hear it when hatred spills from my children. I hear it when selfishness dominates my children's hearts. I hear it when my frustration overtakes me and my patience flies out the window, only to come back in the still of night when small eyelids flutter and mama hearts sink.

I hear it in their questions. I see it in their glances. I see it in the mirror.

One word. One word heavy enough to crush my best intentions. One word sharp enough to pierce through my greatest performance.

FAILURE.

When do you hear that word rattle against your ear, reminding you of how short you've fallen from your perfect standard? When do the voices of the crowd and your mistakes and your would-have-could-have-should-have efforts tell you that you simply don't measure up and your stomach twists up like a pretzel of shame, dipped in anxiety and sprinkled with fear?

Can I tell you something, sweet mama?

It's a lie.

From the pit of Hell.

We are bombarded by lies on a moment-by-moment basis. About our identity. About our womanhood. About our roles as mothers. About our children. The book that told me what to expect when that precious treasure arrived didn't account for a child who hadn't read the book and didn't know the rules.

The friends who told me how children should respond to their mothers forgot to give the memo to my children.

Just like I didn't measure up to my expectations for myself, my kids didn't measure up to my expectations, either. They didn't nurse for long enough. They didn't play together nicely. They didn't act the way I expected them to.

I got caught up in the "mom wins" and "mom fails" game. And on the scale of reality, I soon realized that my failures far outweighed my wins. And it wasn't until I understood the truth that I saw the lie.

What if there aren't wins or fails in motherhood?

What if motherhood is the place where we lay down our religion and pious notions of self-righteousness at the foot of Jesus and fall helplessly in His arms?

What if motherhood is the place where our children see how madly in love with Jesus we are and want to fall in love with Him, too? Not because we're really great moms, but because we have a really great God.

What if motherhood became less of a competition and more of a transformation — where we take our eyes off the measuring scales of perfection and fix our eyes on the One who makes us whole?

And what if motherhood is the place where the great deceiver works overtime to keep our eyes diverted, because he knows an army of mama bears who rise up with nothing to prove can change the world?

Sweet mama, can I tell you something? Motherhood is most definitely the place where the deceiver works overtime. Because he most certainly knows what is at stake. So he feeds us lies, desperate to make us believe anything but the truth — because he knows the truth will set us free.

And free mamas are no joke.

All women, mothers or not, are susceptible to these lies. Motherhood just amplifies it because somehow we've convinced ourselves that we should be enough for our children, and when we're not — because we're not — we feel like failures.

And the enemy snacks on our guilt.

Several months ago, I led a small group of preteen girls in my home. I taught them a little about God, and I learned a lot about Taylor Swift in the process. One week I asked them to write down on a piece of paper the lies they believe about themselves.

Here's what they wrote down:

I am fat.
I will never be pretty because of my freckles.
I am stupid.
Nobody loves me.
No one will ever want to be my friend.
Nobody would miss me if I died.
I will never reach my dreams.
I am invisible.
My hair isn't long enough.
I'm not cool enough.
I don't fit in.
People won't ever accept me.

Sound familiar? These are 10- and 11-year-old girls! One of them is *my* 11-year-old girl. My heart bleeds for them. They should be thinking about unicorns and candy — not that nobody would miss them if they died. And by the way, these are church girls. They've been raised in church. They know the right answers. They know the songs. They've heard the stories.

What is happening to us, girls? What is happening to our daughters, our friends, our world? From our vantage point, we can see the truth. Why in the world would you believe this about yourself? Can't you see how incredibly remarkable you are? Can't you see that your freckles are exactly what make you adorable?

Can't you see that you are perfect just the way you are?

It's so easy to see the lies that someone else is believing as unbelievable, but we are so easily convinced that our own lies are completely and totally true.

Where did this come from? Why can't we recognize the lies hissed in our own ears but can identify them so clearly in another's?

I bet I know what you're thinking. Here she goes. Here comes the inevitable *our world is so awful, stop watching TV and reading magazines because we'll never live up to those false images of perfect women,* blah blah blah.

I could blame it on the Barbies and their tiny waists and giant boobs. I could blame it on Disney and its overemphasis on relationships and unrealistic endings. I could blame it on *boy, what is this world coming to,* the internet and social media. I would do that if I believed this is something new to our daughter's generation. I would do that if I believed this was something new to our generation. I would do it even if I believed it was something new to our mothers' generation.

Oh, sweet mamas! This story goes much further back then all of that. Long before Barbies, Disney and *Vogue,* women were faced with the same battle we face every morning before our feet even hit the floor. Let's let that plastic doll off the hook for just a minute and turn our arrows on the real culprit, shall we? That sneaky snake has been after us from the very beginning, dripping lies into our beautiful, powerful minds.

Because he knows that if he can attack our mind, we'll never move out of the darkness. We'll fear the light. After all, he's right, isn't he?

If they only knew the real me, they'd run for cover. It's safer here in the dark. I'll just stay here a little longer.

And so we remain, hiding in the dark, fighting each other — arguing about things that don't matter — while the enemy gains ground in our hearts, our homes, our churches and our world.

Do you remember what the snake said to beautiful, innocent Eve? Before she ever had another woman to compare herself to. Before she could look at a Barbie and wonder why her boobs weren't shaped like that. Before she could wonder if her husband was looking at another woman, she heard these words, and they sank like cement in her soul. We find her in the garden, the whole of God's fullness, there for the taking. But there's one thing God didn't give her. One fruit she wasn't allowed to eat. The snake slithered up to her, breath heavy on her neck, and asked the question still rattling our souls today.

Did God really say ...?[1]

Can you hear him? Can you hear the pin drop into Eve's innocent heart? That question that pierced through everything she thought she believed and everything she thought she knew?

Did God really say you couldn't eat from any tree in the garden?

Can you feel her heart shudder, her trust crumbling at its quake? Can you hear her pulse pound, her hope splintering at its blow?

Well, now that you mention it, I'm not sure. Now that I'm thinking about it, maybe not. Actually, I wasn't really listening. I was a bit distracted by the naked man walking beside me. Are You sure about that anatomy, God? Looks a little strange to me.

Did God really say that you're okay just the way you are?

Did God really say you don't have to try harder?

Did God really say He loves you? That He was enough and you don't need to go looking in other places to find your worth?

Did He really say it?

Surely being still and knowing He's God isn't enough.

Don't you need to do something?

Do you remember how the snake deceived her? He took God's words and twisted them, convincing Eve that there was something better out there. She just had to go looking for it.

Come over here, Eve. Let me show you what you're missing. You deserve better than this. Poor you, over there with all that boring fruit. It's better over here. You're missing out. Look at how good it is over here.

Poor, poor Eve. Did God really say that He's enough for you? He obviously doesn't want what's best for you. Are you sure He's even really good?

Sound familiar?

Can you see the thoughts racing through Eve's mind? *He's right. I am missing something. Maybe God isn't really enough. Maybe God is holding out on me. Maybe He isn't good after all.*

And if He is, He's certainly not good to me.

Everything Eve needed was already given to her. She had nothing to compare herself with, and yet she fell for the enemy's scheme.

And he convinced her she needed to be more, find more and have more in order to be worth more.

Let's fast forward a few thousand years after our sweet Eve. A man clad in linen garb and dirty sandals stands beside a river, the water lapping against His legs. He's ready to embark on His life's mission. He's ready to save the world.

He enters the river, the crowd gasping as the man who everyone is talking about dips back beneath the murky water. As He rises, robe clinging heavy with the water, this God-in-the-flesh man looks upon the world He came to save. The Spirit descends on Him, and the voice of His Father shouts out to the on-looking world.

"This is My Son, whom I love. With Him I am well pleased."[2]

If God had Facebook there at the Jordan River, He'd be blowing up His feed with the news. I didn't have Facebook to announce my babies' births. Poor things. Nobody even knew how incredible they were. Sometimes I want to have another baby, just so I can see how many people will congratulate me.

Here's my paraphrase to God's announcement:

"Hey there, ya'll! Are you listening? Are you paying attention? This is MY Son! I love Him so much, My heart might just burst! He makes Me so incredibly happy, and if you just look at Him, your day will get a whole lot brighter! I want you to meet Him. I want you to know

Him like I do. He's the greatest thing that ever happened to this earth. And if you just get to know Him, you're going to love Him, too!"

He's the doting Dad, incredibly proud of His Son. This is a full-blown Rafiki-holding-up-Simba-on-the-edge-of-a-rock moment while Mufasa puffs out his chest and shakes his mane. Can you see it? Can you hear His voice radiate through the clouds as a hush washes over the crowd?

But I think the message wasn't as much for the crowd as it was for Jesus. God wanted Jesus to know who He was. He was loved, and His Father was pleased with Him.

Didn't Jesus already know this? Did this man who built the storehouses of snow and breathed fire into the rising sun need to know His worth? Did the Author of Truth need truth spoken into His human heart?

In His tenderness, God knew Jesus would need the reminder in the days ahead. He knew what was coming. He knew Jesus would need to remember.

For the snake, aware of the insecurities that plague humans, only possesses one battle plan.

To lie.

It's in the very next verse that we find Jesus in the depths of the wilderness.[3] He's hungry. It's been 40 days since He's had a bite of anything. He's alone. It's been 40 days since He's seen the face of a friend. And that snake slithers right into that lonely, hungry place where lies waft up like bread fresh from the oven, ready to strike.

Take a look at what he says.

If You are the Son of God, turn these stones into bread.

If You are really who You think You are, bow down to me, and I'll give You the glory You deserve.

If You are the Son of God, jump off this temple, and let's just see if Your Daddy catches You.[4]

Here's what I hear that snake saying to Jesus in the thick of the wilderness.

If You are really the Son of God, then You shouldn't be hungry, should You? Poor You. God must not really love You as much as You thought. If He did, You wouldn't be feeling like this. He would give You what You wanted. You would be full and happy.

If You are really the Son of God, You should get the glory You deserve. The people would acknowledge You. They would cheer for You.

Bow down and worship me, and I'll give You their cheers. I'll give You their applause. Clearly You aren't enough, since they aren't clapping. Do more! Be more! Try more!

If You are really the Son of God, then You wouldn't have to experience the pain that's coming. You must not be who You think You are if You are going to suffer like that. God must have forgotten about You. He wouldn't let someone He loves go through that.

Are You sure He said He's pleased with You?

Are You sure He's enough?

Are You sure You're enough for Him?

Sweet mama, have you heard similar words spoken to that lonely, hungry crack in your heart?

If you are the daughter of the King, then why are you lonely? Why hasn't your King given you what you need? Remember all those unanswered prayers? Poor you. He must not really care about you, or He would give you what you need. You shouldn't have to feel this way. He should have come through for you.

If you are the daughter of the King, people should notice you. Nobody sees you. Nobody loves you. Come over here, and I'll give you some cheers. Look over here, and I'll give you applause. Look at the people. That's where you'll find your worth. Your Daddy must not care all that much, or you would feel better.

If you are the daughter of the King, you wouldn't have to go through this. Didn't your Daddy offer you abundant life? Why is your husband not leading you? Why are your kids so misbehaved? Why does everyone else have so many friends, and you're sitting there all alone?

Jump into this pit over here. Let's just see if Daddy will catch you.

It is no coincidence that God tells Jesus who He is right before this trial. He knows the enemy's battle plan. He's seen the blue prints. He knows the scheme. And now we do, too. We're onto that sneaky snake.

It's time to fight, girls. It's time to stop looking around and comparing ourselves to each other and grip each other's hands as we move forward on the battleground. How cunning of our enemy to convince us to fight each other so we stop fighting him!

Sweet mama, first you must hear your Father speak truth over you. You must abide in His love long enough so that you actually believe what He says. We've been talking about the heartbeat of God — that it beats for you. I know it's hard to believe.

I know you're doubting, trying to cling to the truth but bombarded by the lies.

I've said it over and over again because I'm reminding myself as much as I'm reminding you. You can never defeat the lies unless you know the truth. It's impossible. You will always succumb to the lies until you hear your name with every beat of your Father's heart.

You are a daughter of the Most High. He delights in you. Don't believe me? Don't take my word for it. Listen to what He says about you.

"The Lord delights in those who fear Him, who put their hope in His unfailing love." (Psalm 147:11, NIV)

"For the sake of His great name, the Lord will not reject His people, because the Lord was pleased to make you His own." (1 Samuel 12:22, NIV)

"No more will anyone call you Rejected ... you will no longer be called Ruined.
You'll be called My Delight ... Because God delights in you. As a bridegroom is happy in his bride, so your God is happy with you." (Isaiah 62:3-5, *The Message*)

"The King is wild for you." (Psalm 45:11, *The Message*)

"The King's daughter is all glorious within: her clothing is of wrought gold."
(Psalm 45:13, KJV)

Once you are His, He is pleased with you. A daughter of the King is glorious within. It can't be any other way. It can't be changed or revoked. Why? Because He lives inside you!

Hear Him say it right now.

This is My daughter. I love her. With her I am well pleased.

YOU, sweet mama. You are His daughter. He loves you. And with you He is so very pleased.

But I yelled at my kids this morning!

But I haven't read my Bible in a week!

But I didn't do devotions with my kids before Easter this year!

But I spent too much time on my phone this week and didn't play at the park with my kids!

But I was selfish and I went to Target three times this week instead of giving my money to the poor!

But I ate microwave popcorn for lunch instead of a salad!

This is what most of my years as a mom looked like. Clawing my way through my performance back into God's presence because I thought when I failed at motherhood, I disappointed Him, and when I succeeded, He was pleased. I wasn't trying to earn my way to Heaven. I was trying to earn my way out of His disappointment.

But then I began questioning this performance-driven relationship. At what point is God disappointed? Can I fail five times in a day before He starts shaking His head at me? Do I get 20 chances to get it right? Or is it the first time I mess up that rouses His disappointment? If I have a long quiet time in the morning, is He happier with me than if I miss a day? And if so, what do I need to do to earn His approval back once I've failed?

It was then that I realized that my performance issues weren't just for the applause of people. I thought I needed to perform for God. Not for my salvation — I was far too spiritual to believe I could lose that. No, I was performing for His approval — for His grace in my daily life. Because the truth was I didn't believe it. I couldn't believe He was pleased with me unless my life proved I was worth it.

If the power of grace, regardless of what we've done to deserve it, is enough to get us out of Hell and into Heaven, then why isn't it enough to get us through the day?

The enemy used the same battle plan with Jesus that he used with Eve. He didn't come up with anything new. Sweet mama, his tricks are the same with you and me.

And you can bet your britches he's gonna do the same thing to our kids. He's going to try to get us to believe two things:

1. God must not be good.
2. We must not be loved.

Either God isn't who He says He is, or I'm not who He says I am. And if the snake can get us to believe either of these, then he's got us. Got us good. That's when we look for something other than God to fill the void.

If God isn't good, then we'll look somewhere else. In people. In work. In our circumstances. In relationships, addictions, popularity and revenge. In our children.

Or we start striving. We start trying to earn God's approval through our performance. Trying to sculpt our bodies into a more loveable shape. Trying to forge our hearts into a more loveable nature. Trying to mold ourselves into supermom.

But aren't we supposed to love our children well? Shouldn't we care about our bodies? Is it okay to scream at our kids and spend all our money at Target? These are symptoms, sweet one. Symptoms of a heart spinning for worth — a heart bent with lies.

We can talk all day about how Eve shouldn't have eaten that apple. That was simply the result of a lie whispered to a hungry heart.

We can talk all day about how we shouldn't yell at our kids. But all that does is make us feel guilty — and promise to stop.

My anger, my fear, my need to be more — do more — have more — are symptoms of my insecurity fed by the lies my heart believes.

I should read my Bible, but not because it makes God happy with me. I read my Bible because it's how I remember. It's how I remember that God really is good, despite how I feel. It's how I remember I really am loved, despite how much I've failed.

And when I remember that God really is good, and I really am loved, He does the changing. He does the sculpting and molding — not changing me into supermom, but into who I already am in Him.

> "But whoever did want Him, who believed He was who He claimed and would do what He said, He made to be their true selves, their child-of-God selves." (John 1:12, *The Message*)

I am loved.
I am a daughter of the King.
And when I stop striving for worth, I start living free.

As I write this, I'm fighting a fresh wave of lies. Like trying to stand your ground in the ocean as wave after wave pummels over you — that's how it feels. As soon as I gain my footing, another one slams me back down. I woke up this morning convinced that my words don't matter. Convinced that no one needs anything I have to offer, I told myself to close down shop, put the computer away.

Sometimes the fear is paralyzing.

We're struggling with our oldest daughter right now. Parenting feels arduous and futile at times. I'm worn from trying. I'm frayed from failing. Our home looks like a war zone most evenings. I've prayed for answers and miracles. I've wept more tears than I knew I possessed. This isn't what I imagined my family would look like. I thought my kids would be best friends. They aren't. Not even close. I'm writing a book about motherhood, and I don't know how to reach my own child. Some days I don't know how to put one foot in front of the other.

We've recently moved, and I'm inundated with loneliness. I look around at how happy everyone else seems — how many friends everyone else has — and I feel unlovable and unusable. I feel unseen and forgotten. I'm writing a book about freedom in Christ, and I've forgotten who I am. I've forgotten who He is. What could I possibly have to say to you when I'm drowning in self-doubt as a riptide of lies pulls me out into the sea of despair?

When my heart is cracked and dry from the desert sun, I hear that same question hiss against my ear — *If you are ...*

When life doesn't turn out the way we thought it would, the lies whisper our name. When children rebel and marriages crumble, that snake hisses stories in our ears. When addictions reign and questions lurk, doubt descends. When the Promised Land becomes Never Land, and our failures pull our feet out from under us, the snake is ready to strike. And he convinces us there are only two reasonable explanations for life's cruelty.

God is not good.

We are not loved.

And I fell for it. Maybe God isn't all that good. Maybe He doesn't want the best for me. Maybe He's holding out on me. Maybe He isn't who He says He is. And maybe it's true that I'm not enough. I don't have what it takes. Maybe I'm not who He says I am. Maybe I am as unlovable as I feel.

And that's when I get it. I remember Eve, hungry for more when she already has everything. I remember Jesus, full to the brim when He's 40 days starving. And I remember that snake, and I'm onto his plan.

Hearts are on the line. My daughter's heart. We're focusing on her symptoms. I can tell her until I'm blue in the face to stop lashing out at her sister. But that's not the problem. She's hungry for Jesus. And hungry hearts always lash out until they are full. My husband's heart. I can beg him until my heart bleeds dry to be a better husband. Just like I can beg myself to be a better mom, right? The enemy only has one trick up his sleeve!

He's lying to my husband.

He's lying to my children.

He's lying to me.

And I've been fighting the wrong enemy.

What lies are you being fed today? How is the enemy sneaking through those hungry cracks in your heart, offering you over-sized helpings of doubt? How are your insecurities ruling your days?

Let's look at the symptoms you would love to get rid of.

Anger?

Bitterness?

Shame?

Hopelessness?

Fear?

Addiction?

Jealousy?

Those are merely symptoms. There's something else going on underneath the surface. And we're so susceptible as moms. The snake knows our hearts ache for our children. He knows our weaknesses. He knows we want to be good moms. He knows we wonder if we're enough.

And he knows we so easily believe we're not.

We have a friend who grew up with a pet boa constrictor. For some ridiculous reason, he chose to allow this creature into his bed at night. I don't know about you, but I'd need more than a few margaritas to let a snake in my bed. Often, he would wake up to find the snake stretched out beside him, its slimy scales pressed close against his body. Sounds sweet, doesn't it?

The snake was measuring itself against him, checking for inadequacy — testing for weakness. The snake was sizing up its owner, checking to see who was bigger, waiting for the moment when it could wrap tight around him, squeezing the very life from his body.

We've been sized, sweet mama, and that snake who seeks only to steal and destroy strikes right where he knows he can get us. In our failures, the lies slither up beside us. When we lie awake at night, minds racing and hearts aching, they stretch out, pressing close against our hearts — proving how much we don't measure up.

If you feel strangled by failure, it's because you've let that snake think he's bigger than you. You've let that snake tell you you're not enough. You've let the lies coil tight around your heart, suffocating from the pressure, because you've forgotten the truth.

When you're pressed close against the heartbeat of Jesus, the snake slinks away to hide as you stretch out tall in your true identity. It's the snake who can't measure up — not you.

There are many lies we believe as moms. These are the lies I've heard the most:

You aren't a good mom.
You're fat.
You're ugly.
You're not enough.
You've ruined your kids.
Your kids are going to make the same mistakes you did.
Your kids are going to hate you one day.
You're a failure.
Your mistakes are too great.
You are too scared.
You are too broken.
God is disappointed in you.

You've been sized, sweet one, by a snake — the accuser — the great deceiver. The question is, how are you sizing yourself?

If you're measuring yourself by the word of the snake, then you'll always think you've failed. That's his plan. If you're measuring yourself by other moms, then you'll always try to perform. If you're sizing yourself by some ridiculous standard you think will give you worth, you'll never be tall enough to reach it.

But if you're sizing yourself by truth, by God's measurements, you'll realize He already took care of your shortcomings. If you're measuring yourself based on the fact that you are His daughter, He loves you and with you He is pleased, you don't have to live up to any standard.

You're already loved.

He's not surprised by your weaknesses. He's not disgusted by your failures. And He's the One who's transforming you into who He sees when He looks at you.

What lies are fueling your symptoms? And when did they start? Remember those sweet baby girls in my living room? Those 11-year-olds weighed down with ancient lies. The lies you and I believe didn't start big, and they didn't begin the moment Mama became our name. The enemy spoon-feeds us as little girls. And he increases our helpings as we grow. He's so cunning that we don't even recognize the lies. They become a part of us, ingrained within the lining of our hearts. And the crazy part? He doesn't even have to stuff it down our throats. We help ourselves to the all-you-can-eat buffet of deception spread out before us.

When did you first believe the lie that you have to perform for God? When did you first believe the lie that you're not enough? Why does the fruit of performance look so tasty? Why does the promise of applause sound so inviting? When did you first feel like your body wasn't as beautiful as someone else's? When did you first feel like your kids didn't measure up to someone else's? When did you first feel like you failed as a mom?

Where have you come from, sweet mama? We must first ask ourselves this question before we can find out where we are going.

It's not Barbie's fault. It's not the evil world's fault. It's the snake's fault, and it's time for us to start fighting the real enemy!

Jesus said the truth would set us free.[5] It's the key, dear one. It's the answer. It's where we're headed next, friend.

Let's blow this joint. Let's make like Houdini and bust out of these chains. That snake's got nothing on us. And the next time he tries to slither his way around your heart, pressing close to size you up, he'll realize that he doesn't stand a chance. Because you, sweet mama, know that your God is good, and you are indeed so very loved.

And by the way ... snakes that stay in their cages at night can't size up their owners. Don't let the snake in your bed, honey. For goodness' sake, stop inviting him in.

Digging Deeper

1. Do you believe God is pleased with you?

2. What symptoms are you experiencing right now that you want to get rid of?

3. Are you treating the symptoms or the cause?

4. What lies do you believe about yourself right now?

5. When did those lies start?

6. What lies are you believing about God?

7. How are you measuring yourself right now? By the word of the snake? By your standard? By other moms?

8. What lies are your children believing about themselves right now?

Chapter 7
The Spanx of Truth

There's no toilet paper in the house, and apparently I'm the only one who's noticed. How long has it been since the kids used toilet paper? Days? And nobody said a word? I try not to think about the implications of what that means. The kids went to school today with their underwear inside out because I haven't done the laundry. I try not to connect the dots between the lack of toilet paper and the wearing of dirty underwear.

The refrigerator is a ghost town, so we stopped by Walgreens and grabbed Lunchables on our way to school. I'm not sure what the children ate for breakfast. Probably leftover Easter candy.

The kitchen looks like the cabinets threw up every dish we own all over the counter. Poor cabinets. They must not be feeling well today.

Something rotten is growing arms and legs in the sink, and the smell makes me want to lose my breakfast like the cabinets lost their dishes. But I'm distracted by the obstacle course of shoes blocking my way to the door. Apparently I'm the only one who's noticed that, as well.

The trash is spilling over the top of the garbage can, and some kind of suspicious liquid is dripping down the sides. I try closing the lid, but it keeps popping back up, like a jack-in-the-box on steroids. Apparently I'm the only one who's noticed.

The 7-year-old asked me why my stomach looks like there's a baby in it. I told her it was because I ate too much for dinner last night, but I was thinking, *It's because of you, sweet one, and thank you so much for that!*

I like a clean house, and I plan to do laundry sometime today. I'll stop by the store and grab some toilet paper and enough food to keep everyone from starving this week. I might even cook dinner tonight. I'll help with homework and break up fights when the kids get home from school. I'll kiss scraped knees and wipe dirt-smudged tears from faces. I'll tuck little bodies snug under wooly blankets and kiss chubby cheeks soft under moonlit skies.

Tomorrow I'll do it all again. I'll show up to this thing called mother-hood. And tomorrow it might look different.

I'll make lunches with fresh food from the fridge. I'll make scrambled eggs for their little growing brains. They'll eat all their veggies, and we'll be on time for school.

I'll re-clean the kitchen and wipe milk off the counters. I'll play catch and read stories. I'll remind them to brush their teeth for the thousandth time and ask them why they can't remember.

I'll wonder if it's all worth it, and then I'll look on their sleeping faces and remember it is.

I might go to the gym, or I might meet a friend for lunch. And if all the stars align, I might even eat a salad.

I'll lose my temper and look deep into their eyes and ask for forgiveness. I'll kiss wind-blown hair and rub tired backs. I might bake cookies with them or let them watch too many episodes on Netflix. I might make a healthy, well-balanced dinner or hide in the pantry eating a bag of mini-snickers.

I'll show up, break down, lose my mind, love them hard, lose my mind again and show up the next day, anyway. Because that's motherhood.

And through it all, I will have a choice to make. A choice that will determine whether each day is a success or a failure. On the days we use underwear for toilet paper, and on the days I make lasagna from scratch, I have the same choice. I can believe the lies or cling to the truth. I have the choice to measure myself by my performance and the word of the snake or to measure myself by the Word of my God.

The choice is always ours, sweet mama. In the mountains of laundry. In the *I'm sorry I yelled at you* conversations. In the Pinterest flops and picture day fails. In the overdue library books and back-seat tantrums (the kids' or ours). In the homemade valentines and freshly baked bread. In blueberry muffins fresh from the oven and leftover Easter candy on the way out the door. On the days when our kids are friends and quote Scripture to strangers, and the days when they fight like crazy and we hope the neighbors can't hear.

In this place called motherhood, where the mediocre becomes sacred and hearts learn the rhythm of grace, we all have the same choice to make. Will we believe the lies or cling to the truth?

It's just a matter of where we are looking. Looking in the mirror at shame. Looking to the people for applause. Looking to the standard for worth. Or looking up into the face of truth.

In the battle for hearts, truth wins.

Every. Single. Time.

There's a battle raging for your heart, sweet mama. If you're tired, the weight of the world on your shoulders, there's only one thing that will set you free.

It's truth, luv. And it's free.

It's the face looking back at you when you look into the mirror of grace instead of the mirror of shame. It's the King who sweat crimson tears in the garden that night, bearing the weight of your sin and shame on His shoulders so you could stand tall.[1]

What's weighing you down, sweet one? What's that snake been whispering in your ear?

There's a woman in the Bible who quite literally carried the weight of the world on her shoulders. We find her in Luke 13, carrying a boulder of pain on her back.[2] Luke tells us she was bent over double, not hunched over a bit from poor posture. She was bent completely double — her face at her knees. Like if you and I could actually stretch like the workout videos tell us to and reach our toes. She'd been like this for 18 years. It'd been 18 years since someone had looked her in the eyes. Eighteen years since she'd felt the embrace of a friend. Eighteen years since she'd watched the clouds roll by, danced at a wedding, made love or watched children play in the grass.

Scholars believe that this woman suffered from a form of arthritis where a person begins to suffer from pain in her lower back, so she bends over just enough to relieve the pain. After time, the bones fuse together, and she can't stand up straight again.

The problem is, the relief doesn't last. The pain continues, so she bends over just a little bit more. The bones fuse in that position, too. Until, finally, she's bent double — and there's nowhere else to go.³

Can you imagine her plight? Eighteen years. This was all she knew — this weight heavy on her shoulders. Her sickness became her very existence — her identity wrapped up in the invisible chains that held her body captive.

Luke introduces us to her in the synagogue. Who would have thought we'd run into her at church? She was religious. She showed up, week after week. But she wasn't free.

And then Jesus showed up.

He saw her, and in that moment, He not only saw where she was; He saw where she'd been. He saw each plummet. Every trip in the dust. He'd heard every question and doubt. And as He looked on her, He called her close.

*Dear woman, you are set free!*⁴

Do you see the look of love in His eyes? Can you see His heart ache for her plight? How precious she is to her Savior. He has more for her in this life. More than she can experience bent over staring at the ground. More than she could ever know with her face in the dust. Jesus sets her free and calls her to a new life she never dreamed possible.

*Immediately she stood up straight. And oh, how she praised God.*⁵

Can you imagine the look on her face when she stood up for the first time in 18 years? Can you picture her twirling, arms stretched to the sky, as the wind blew fresh on her face? Can you hear her laughing? Can you see her running to Jesus, kneeling at His feet in such gratitude — such awe and amazement? The weight — gone. In an instant, she was set free, life forever changed.

Sweet mama, Jesus sees you. He sees where you have been. He sees every plummet, every best intention, every failure and every broken promise to yourself. And He's calling you close. Can you see the look of love in His eyes? We're not all that different from this sweet woman. Many of us are weighed down, bent over with bitterness, shame, guilt or fear.

Remember that snake? Remember his plan? What lies have you weighed down today? What disappointments and unmet expectations — of yourself, of other people or of God — are pinning you down?

When the lies come, weighing heavy on our hearts, we lean just a little bit forward to find relief, don't we?

Every time you compare yourself to other moms and convince yourself you're not good enough, you lean forward with guilt.

Every time you promise yourself you'll do better and fail, you lean forward with shame.

Every time you believe God is disappointed in you, you lean forward in fear.

When betrayals sink their knives into our backs, we lean just a little bit forward to stop the pain. And before we know it, we're bent double, weighed down by boulders of shame, regret, disappointment and fear.

Until there's nowhere else to go.

It's no wonder when that snake slithers up, sizing us up with lies as smooth as glass, we feel like his measurements are accurate. If we're bent over, shackled with guilt and fear, how can we possibly see how tall we really are?

Jesus set our sweet friend free. Doesn't this sound lovely? I know you long for freedom. You've probably asked for it — maybe even begged. But you still aren't sure. Maybe you even believe you've been set free. You've heard Jesus call you close, and you've felt His healing touch. So why do you still feel weighed down?

Why do your steps feel heavy-laden, doubts crowding your mind?

In the Bible, this woman's story ends with her freedom. She praises God and goes on her merry way. Off to her happily-ever-after ending. But I can't stop thinking about her. And one question burns in my mind as I imagine the rest of her story.

What happened when she went home?

Even though the Bible doesn't tell us anything after her brief encounter with Jesus, we know her life was never the same. But what happened when she stepped back into reality and everything now looked upside down? Her story didn't end with her freedom. That was only the beginning. I bet she danced and sang and skipped all the way home. But what happened when she walked in the door and realized that her life revolved around her sickness? Did she bump her head on the door, forgetting that she was now standing tall? What happened when she went to cook her dinner and remembered that her pots and pans were still down on the ground?

Did she miss the view from way down there?

She would need to completely reorganize her life. Everything about her previous life functioned for her as a bent-over woman. A woman standing tall in freedom requires a different way of living. And it would take time for her to live fully in her freedom.

Eighteen years as a prisoner makes one think like a prisoner.

I wonder if she ever bent over to pick something up, only to remember she didn't have to live like that anymore. I wonder if she ever found herself looking at the ground because she forgot she could now look people in the eye. She would have to continually remind herself that she was no longer bound. She was free.

But she had to think free in order to live free.

I wonder if she ever thought that maybe it would just be a whole lot easier to keep things as they were before. She knew how life worked down there. She knew what to expect down there. And there's a good chance, when faced with the reality of living tall, she wondered if living small would be a whole lot safer.

Freedom requires that we reorganize our lives. We have to change the way we think in order to live fully in the freedom we've been given. This woman could have gone home and realized that it was too much work to change the way she'd been thinking. If she left everything the same, she'd still live bent over. Can you imagine?

How sad to be able to see the sky but continue staring at the dust.

How unfortunate to be able to dance but stay bound with imaginary chains.

How tragic to be created to live tall but choose to live small.

Yet you and I do it all the time. Jesus set us free. He called us dear and freed us from our shame. We don't have to live bent over any longer. But if you've believed a lie about yourself for 20, 30, 40 years, then you've learned to function bent over. And it's going to take some training in order to live standing straight. It means we have to rearrange our lives. We have to learn a new way of thinking.

But maybe it's just too much work to change the way we think. Maybe it's easier to keep staring at the dust instead of gazing at the sky.

Maybe it's safer to live small than to live tall.

Paul talks about putting on the armor of God in the book of Ephesians.[6] This chapter irritates me. He sounds so vague, and for the longest time, I didn't understand most of what Paul was saying. He talks about this belt of truth as if everyone is a soldier in the Roman army.

I try as hard as I can to not wear a belt. Let's be honest here, post-baby bellies need all the help they can get, right? A belt on my belly looks like an extra roll of fat. No, thank you. If my pants fall down, that means I'm super skinny, right? I'll stay away from the belt then, thank you very much. Even those wide belts my cute friends wear over their dresses don't work on me. They just push the fat beneath the belt so that it looks like I'm saving some leftover lunch in the pouch down there. So it irritated me that Paul tells me to put on the belt of truth. That's annoying, Paul. Say something I can relate to, buddy!

It was during those dark days of motherhood, hidden there in the cocoon, that I realized how bent over I was with shame and fear. I felt like a failure in all areas, weighed down and burnt out. As God began pressing truth into my heart — those secret treasures whispered in my ear — I began doing research into this belt business. I couldn't shake the fact that it was important, so I tried to shake my annoyance and find out what was so special about this belt.

For a Roman soldier, the belt was the most important piece of armor. It wasn't just to keep their pants up (they didn't wear pants). It was the piece that held everything together. It kept everything in place.[7] The belt anchored the breastplate. The belt secured the weapons. It wasn't a fashion accessory. It was the foundation of the armor. If a soldier didn't wear the belt, there was no reason to wear any other piece of the armor. It meant the difference between life and death.

I still can't relate to Roman soldiers. But I can relate to something else that's pretty good at holding things together. Someone who had probably popped out a few babies invented something called Spanx. For those of us who didn't ever fit back into our pre-pregnancy clothes and now care very little for comfort — we love us some Spanx!

It's a beautiful thing when things that fall out can magically be held together again.

A few years ago, my husband and I attended a gala for his work. I picked out a sexy black dress, pulled on my Spanx and thought I looked pretty darn fabulous. That is until I posed for pictures in the middle of a bunch of 25-year-olds and realized none of them had double chins.

The dinner went longer than expected. For hours, I sat at the table while someone onstage droned on about the exhilarating world of selling health insurance. As I grew tired — and rather bored — I started to lean forward a bit.

The problem with Spanx is that when you lean over, they dig into your gut, squeezing your dinner back up into your esophagus. I had to sit up straight in order to keep my mashed potatoes from revisiting my plate.

I can't relate to a Roman belt holding up armor, but I can relate to Spanx that hold my stretched and flabby belly in place. So, instead of putting on the belt of truth, sweet mama, I want us to put on the Spanx of truth.

If we are held together in truth, when we start to lean forward, we're reminded how uncomfortable a life bent over feels. Truth reminds us that we were made to live standing straight — confident in who we are in Christ.

Confident that we really are who He says we are — even if our lives don't completely look like it yet.

The problem is, Spanx aren't comfortable. I don't know about you, but I don't lie around watching Netflix in my Spanx. I save them for special occasions. It's far more comfortable to wear my fat pants so there's more room when I feel like indulging in a chocolatey morsel.

Truth is uncomfortable. If you have believed a lie about yourself for most of your time as a mother, then it's going to be uncomfortable to believe something else. We've been trained to believe that feeling bad about ourselves is spiritual. We've been trained to believe that a true sign of humility is to beat ourselves up and try harder tomorrow.

Lies are comfortable. Lies feel good. Otherwise, why on earth would we believe them?

That's the catch. We have to reorganize the way we think. Truth sets us free, but only when truth is what we think about. And the more we think about truth, the more we'll be able to distinguish the lies.

So how do we do it? What does this actually look like? If God knows the blue prints for the snake's plan, then it shouldn't come as a surprise that He gave us a battle plan of our own. The thing is, sweet one, God doesn't want you to live bent over. Despite what you were told growing up. Despite how you feel about yourself today. God wants to set you free.

And He knows exactly how to do it.

Be transformed by the renewing of your minds.[8]

Clinging to truth is how we reorganize our lives. This is the process of transformation. The time it takes for experience to catch up with reality. Jesus says that if you've been set free, you are free indeed.[9] There's no going back. If He calls you dear and sets you free, you don't have to live bent over any longer.

But you can choose to live bent over because it's more comfortable. You can choose to keep your thinking the same and nothing about your life will change. Your life won't look any different because you aren't thinking any differently.

Want your life to look different? Then think differently.

Like the woman who had to go home and change the way she thought in order to live free. She had to think in the way that reflected her reality, even if she didn't feel that way yet.

You and I, sweet mama, need to change the way we think.

This woman was already healed. She was already free. But it would take time for her experience to catch up with her reality.

You are already gold, sweet mama. You don't have to waste your efforts trying to spin yourself into anything else. But if you think of yourself as worthless, unlovable and broken, then you will live that way. You will keep living bent over with a back that's straight as steel. We stand in the truth that sets us free and live out of the reality that makes us whole.[10] If you think of yourself as the delight of your Abba's heart, then you will live that way — and you'll laugh at the thought of staring at dust because you've caught a glimpse of the sun!

Stop looking at the ground, and look up to the sky! Stop thinking you can't walk, and start dancing! Stop letting that snake in your head, and stand up straight, believing you are worth looking someone in the eye!

Paul tells us why it's so important to arm ourselves with truth. He actually did know what he was talking about after all.

We need the armor so that when the battle is over, we'll still be standing.[11] He knew how easy it is to knock someone down who's bent over. He knew that we'll never change this world when we're stuck with our faces in the dust.

And that snake knows it, too.

Why do you think he's trying so hard to keep us down there? Truth is what keeps us together. So when the battle is over, dust settling upon the ground, we'll still be standing.

When there's no toilet paper, the cabinets are throwing up dishes, creatures are growing in our sinks and our best is never enough — we'll still be standing.

When our kids behave, our houses are clean, our dinners are eaten and our prayers are answered — we'll still be standing.

And together we'll link arms, marching brave across the battlefield — breathless and bleeding at times, but there to pick each other up.

And we'll show up day after day. Because that's motherhood. And we're in this thing together.

Digging Deeper

1. How does guilt, shame or fear weigh you down?

2. In what ways are you living "bent over" right now?

3. Is it easier for you to believe lies than believe truth about yourself?

4. In what ways are you choosing to live bent over because it's easier?

5. How do you need to rearrange the way you think?

6. Do you feel safer living small than living tall?

7. What habits do you need to rearrange that are keeping you from living tall?

Chapter 8

The Truth, the Whole Truth and Nothing but the Truth

The 4-year-old lies prostrate on the kitchen floor, dust mites and old Cheerios her only companions. Her sun-kissed hair reaches out in all directions, leaves and twigs peeking through the wisps, as if a bird attempted to make a nest in those golden locks. Her blue eyes flash like sapphires, burning bright with anger. The only sign of her silken cheeks are the paths forged by tears through the dirt smeared across her face. She's been playing hard in the fresh summer air, looking for bugs and adventure. Little tokens of summer to hold in her tiny hands. She came home holding a heart full of disappointment instead.

As her tantrum subsides, I ask what happened. With shoulders heaving, lungs gasping, she tells me her story. It's one I've heard before. Words thrown out in carelessness land heavy on the hearts that catch them.

"What did they say, luv?" I slip in through the sobs.

"They didn't want to play with me. They said I don't even know how to do anything." She turns her face away, arms crossed and head hung low.

I take her dirty chin in my hand and turn her face to mine. I look into those sapphire eyes and see the look I've seen in the mirror before. "Is that true?" I ask, wiping away the dirt from her tear-stained face.

"They hate me. They never want to play with me. They always are mean. I'm not good at anything. Not even nobody likes me!"

My precious 4-year-old, weighed down with those ancient lies. It's so easy to see them for what they really are in someone else. And to see the truth as plain as day.

Stand up, precious one. Look to the sky!

"What's the truth, sweet girl? People are going to say things. You get to choose what you believe. You're believing a lie right now. We have to exchange it with the truth."

Those sapphire eyes look up at me, pools of hopelessness forming in their depths.

"There is no truth!" she screams. And I hear the hollow cry of a heart desperate for hope yet scared to death she'll never find it.

And I see myself in those eyes. How many times have I said the same thing? It's so hard to see the truth when you're lying face down in the dust.

In the battle for hearts, truth wins. Every. Single. Time.

But first we must know the truth. And then we have to believe it.

Only then will it ever set us free.

The Truth About God

In 2013, the word "miracle" flashed across the despair in my soul like lightning across a black sky. This would be the year of miracles. A promise given to a desperate heart.

The word came to me as I cried out to God for answers — begging Him to set me free from the darkness of my cocoon.

I always ask God what the next year will hold. He always tells me, although I never see it fulfilled until the end. So, when I asked Him in January what my year would hold, His whisper rang clearly in my heart.

MIRACLE.

Five situations in my life desperately needed a miracle. Clinging to the promise of THE miracle worker, I hoped expectantly that each of these situations would be redeemed in the year 2013.

So I believed. This would be the year of miracles.
So I prayed. This would be the year of miracles.
So I waited. This would hopefully be the year of miracles.
So I grew impatient. Maybe this wouldn't be the year of miracles.
So I gave up hope. This clearly wasn't the year of miracles.

One year later, each of these situations seemed more hopeless than before. God felt distant. Silent. Inattentive to my prayers. Uncaring of my plight.

I begged God to do something. Show me Your power! I believe! I believe You can part the Red Sea. I believe You can tear down the walls of Jericho. I believe You can slay a giant. I believe that You can conquer any enemy that comes against me.

But what I need You to do right now is perform a couple miracles in my life!!!

And then came the whispers of doubt.

If He cared about me, He would do this for me. Why would He give me a promise only to leave me disappointed? These miracles weren't just shallow wishes. Not some things that I thought would make my life happier or easier. These were heartbreaking, gut-wrenching problems that were tearing my life apart.

One Sunday in July, a stranger in church told me God wanted me to read the book of John. I scoffed with doubt. God hadn't spoken a word in months, and now suddenly He was going to tell some guy I didn't know that I needed to read my Bible?

But strangers with messages from God have a way of getting into your head. I went home and read the book of John. In chapter 4, verse 48, Jesus asks the people a question that shot straight into my disappointment. And that double-edged sword cut open and laid bare all of my misconceived ideas and warped view of God.

"Will you never believe in Me unless you see miraculous signs and wonders?"

And then the whisper that was silent for so long broke through the barricade around my heart.

My child, for a year and a half, I've been teaching you that you don't have to perform for Me. But why do I have to perform for you? You don't need to perform to earn My favor. Why must I perform to earn your trust? You don't need to perform to be deserving of My blessing. Why must I perform to be deserving of your praise? You don't need to perform to win My presence. Why must I perform to win your heart?

Like fingers of dawn drawing back the curtain of night, the words peeled away the doubt clenched tight around my heart. In that moment, I had a choice to make.

If I didn't need to perform for God, did God need to perform for me?

Remember that snake? Remember his plan? He wants us to believe that God is not good and He cannot be trusted. That somehow God is holding out on us, dangling a carrot in front of us as we chase it in vain. And that He finds pleasure in watching us struggle.

When we trust in who God says He is — not in the God we've conjured up in our minds — He'll sweep us off our feet. He's not the God we think He should be — He's so much bigger than our small minds can fathom. When we discover who God is — the real God He reveals to us in his Word — then He is ready and willing to perform a miracle. But what we might find is that the miracle He produces is what takes place within us — not around us.

The heart that believes in His goodness when nothing good is happening around us.

The heart that is whole when life breaks into pieces.

The faith that stands firm when dreams are shattered.

The strength to keep moving when the way is shrouded in darkness.

These are the miracles that God will perform when we are ready to receive them. But these are the miracles that happen because we want HIM and not what He will do for us. These are the miracles that part Red Seas, tear down walls, slay giants, defeat armies, release captives, raise the dead, open the eyes of the blind and calm the raging storm. These are the miracles that awaken a soul that has too long slept waiting for a miracle.

Of course I couldn't hear my Father's voice during those months.

We will never know His heart when our gaze is fixed on His hand.

I believe in THE great miracle worker, and I won't stop believing that He will redeem the brokenness around me. But for now, I rejoice, because He is redeeming the brokenness within me.

But it's only when I know the truth of who He is that I can rest in His character.

Jesus' disciples had a hard time trusting in God's character, too. They wanted the miracles. They wanted proof that God was *for* them. Jesus knew the road for His friends wouldn't be easy. Some days, the miracles would blow them away in awe. Other days, the hardships would blow them away in fear. Would they stand firm when the miracles fell silent? Would they stay because they knew His heart and not just His hand?

Jesus asked them the question that would make all the difference.

Who do you say that I am?[1]

Who was Jesus to them? Was He the bread-multiplying, water-walking, fish-catching, storm-calming, dead-raising miracle worker they wanted Him to be? Or was He the heart-freeing, fear-crushing, life-altering, chain-breaking, comfort-wrecking miracle worker they needed Him to be?

I ask you the same question Jesus asked His disciples. Who do *you* say He is?

Is God a fluffy white teddy bear, great for cuddling when you feel down? Is He a genie you ask to appear when you need something? Is He someone you go to church to "get"? Is He big enough for your dreams? Is He big enough for your brokenness? Is He the very air you breathe?

Who is He, beyond what you want Him to do for you? Can you stand with Moses and say, "Even if the Promised Land never comes, Your presence is enough, God!"?[2]

Even if the miracles never come, Your presence is enough.

Even if the storm rages on, Your presence is enough.

Every time you believe a lie about God, you will bend over just a little bit more. The disappointments of life are too heavy, and they will weigh you down until you can't see the path in front of you anymore. The storm will knock you over, because it's pretty easy to knock down someone who's bent over. When Ryan bends over to check the chemicals in our pool, I have to restrain myself from pushing him in. And I like the guy. Imagine what it's like for that snake who hates your guts?

If you're living bent over, like Eve, the fruit will suddenly look tasty because you're convinced God is holding out on you. You will think you deserve better than what He has given, and you will look for something or someone else to fill the emptiness within.

So what does it look like to put on the Spanx of truth?

Get to know Jesus. Wrap your mind and heart in His character, so when the snake comes a'calling, you can keep a'singing. Like when you turn up the radio in the car loud enough so you can't hear the whining in the back seat (am I the only one?).

When the voice of truth rings louder than the lies, you will stand firm.

That's what Paul says the point of the armor is. So that when the battle is over, we'll still be standing!

I know what you're thinking. *Finally! Here's something I can do.* You've been waiting for the list, haven't you? The to-do list that will make you feel better because you've had a part to play.

Of course you have a part to play! Why on earth would God want a relationship with you if He didn't want you to participate? But this isn't a to-do list. This isn't a go-spend-two-hours-on-your-knees game plan. This isn't a stop-doing-the-dishes-so-you-can-read-your-Bible-for-five-hours plan. Some days it might look like that. Some days you might need to stop everything and lie in the grass as God reveals Himself to you in the breeze. But this isn't about carving time out of your day *for* God as much as it is about realizing that you are *in* Christ all of the time.

Yes, the Bible is God's Word, but you are not closer to Him when you read it. You are just as close to Him when you're washing the dishes. It's not about how much "time" we spend with Jesus. It's about realizing that every moment of every day we are in Him and He is in us. It's the awareness of His presence in our time that causes us to stand firm when the storm whooshes by. It's the anchor of truth we cling to when waves crash overhead. It's the voice that tells us He's good when our circumstances say He's not.

We stand firm because we know Him — His heart, His presence and His faithfulness.

American author and priest Brennan Manning writes, "The Christ within who is our hope of glory is not a matter of theological debate of philosophical speculation. He is not a hobby, a part-time project, a good theme for a book or a last resort when all human effort fails. He is our life, the most real fact about us. He is the power and wisdom of God dwelling within us."[3]

If you are a child of God, then you are in Christ and He is in you.[4] He doesn't come and go. We don't go to church to get more of Him. We don't memorize Scripture because it makes us more holy.

But we do get to know Him better. And we'll only trust Him if we know Him.

How did Jesus' disciples get to know Him? They walked with Him. They talked with Him. They lived life with Him, inviting Him into every aspect of their lives. They invited Him into their ordinary, and in return they experienced the extraordinary. That's what happens when you get to know the real God, not the disappointed God you've fabricated in your mind. Not the angry God you've heard about. The REAL God who moved Heaven and earth to be with you — because He can't stand to be away from you — and who wants to invade your darkness with His light. He wants to set you free from your shame, your guilt and your fear. He didn't come to accuse you, He came to redeem you!

Read your Bible to remember who He is, not to get more holy.

Read your Bible because your Father has a secret to tell you, not because He'll love you more.

Read your Bible because God's heart will sweep you off your feet, not because He'll be disappointed if you don't.

Memorize God's Word because it's your sword against the snake, not because it makes you more spiritual.

Write the truths about God's character all over your house so that truth outshouts the lies, not so you look like a Christian to the neighbors.

But then, live life with Him. Talk to Him while you fold laundry. Picture Him singing over you when you nurse your babies in the still of night. Write truth all over the wall next to the toilet. And if that's the only quiet time you get in a day, then that's okay.

Don't you see the difference? God beckons us, "Taste and see that I am good."[5]

He is good. He is strong. And He is so very faithful.

In the battle for hearts, truth wins.

Every. Single. Time.

The Truth About You

Who are you, sweet mama? Without the expectations and applause. Without your kids, your husband, your job or your ministry. Who are you?

I'm going to say it again. You are loved. Your Abba's heart beats for you.

Are you weighed down today with guilt? Guilt isn't from your Father. It's from the snake.

Does this mean we can do whatever we want and sin doesn't matter? Absolutely not! The Holy Spirit convicts us of our righteousness.[6] He reminds us that we are holy, loved, free, unashamed, cleansed, righteous, redeemed, healed, blameless and good.

When we wallow in self-pity, He tells us, *That's not who you are.* When we're selfish and angry, He whispers, *Remember who you are.*

When we remember our righteousness in Christ, sin doesn't satisfy. The pleasures of this world don't glitter. The applause and pats on the back aren't what we long for. The places where we find worth don't look as appealing.

If the enemy's plan is to lie to us, then the only way to beat him is with truth. All. Day. Long.

As God opened my eyes to His love for me, binding up my broken heart with grace, I realized something else — a whole heart has room for others.

When you live loved, you can give love.

The more I saw God's heart beating for me, the more I realized how it beats for others, as well. God gave me a passion to reach the girls in the strip clubs with His wild grace, so I started a ministry in Colorado Springs called Spoken For. Once a month, beneath a blanket of stars, a friend and I visited the clubs with one goal in mind — to tell the girls how much God loved them.

Don't get me wrong, I would have gladly danced on that stage, but they wouldn't let me wear my Spanx. Only one man wants to see this body without my Spanx on, so I wore a sweater and talked with the girls instead. One man complimented my sweater, which I found somewhat sweet and quite a bit strange, considering my surroundings.

We went into the clubs, offering small gifts. The gifts were peace offerings — an attempt to bridge the gap between our different worlds, just down the street from each other and yet worlds apart.

Isn't that how it often is with the hurting and the healed? Those with the cure stay sick while the sick look desperately for the cure.

The gifts were small — nail polish, makeup or jewelry. We did learn that scarves did not make good gifts. Scarves make great props.

We knew they didn't need our gifts, but we hoped our small gesture could offer these girls a small glimpse of the God who gives lavishly to any who call on His name. They couldn't believe that "church" girls would take the time to tell them they matter. We stayed for hours, hearing their stories and listening to their pain. For many of them, this was the last stop before the streets — a final attempt to salvage some of their dignity. Drugs, suicide, poverty, abuse — all etched across their stories, threads of hopelessness weaved throughout generations.

They confided their dreams to us, whispers in the dark of the lives they dreamed of as little girls. And I realized how the same thread weaves through my story, tying us all together in this journey called life.

I saw a lot of things in my time in the strip clubs. Things forever imprinted in my mind. Some I wish I could forget. Others I pray I won't. But what I remember the most is the look on the girls' faces after they danced. With their performance masks down, that armor shielding their hearts set aside, I watched them hiding in the corner counting their dollar bills. For many of them, dancing made them feel worth something. Tightly clasping their payment, as if it would be taken far more easily than it was given, they slipped away into the night with a tangible measurement of their worth.

I wanted to grab their sweet faces and tell them, "Sweet, precious woman, you are worth so much more than a couple of dollars!"

But then I thought about myself and so many women I know.

Where do we find our worth?

In our kids?

In our performance?

In our Facebook posts and applause from the crowd?

In our mom-wins and Pinterest success?

In our ministries and jobs?

In our bodies and social circles?

These are mere dollars compared to how much you are worth to God.

Oh, sweet, precious mama, you are worth so much more than a couple of dollars!

My beautiful friends who dance for worth under the neon lights, measuring your worth by the money earned, you are worth so much more than a couple of dollars. My beautiful friends who dance under the shiny lights of performance, measuring your worth by the applause gained, you are worth so much more than a couple of dollars.

We aren't so very different, are we? All women, desperate to belong — to be worth something. Yes, we find our worth in different places, but Jesus is the only One who can satisfy our hungry hearts. He's the only One who can fill the cracks and make us whole.

Where are you finding your worth today, sweet mama? In truth? Or are you weighed down, believing the lies of the snake that you don't measure up and you need to try harder?

Every time you believe a lie, you bend over just a little bit more. Every time you allow a wound to fester, you bend over just a little bit more.

No wonder we walk around feeling like crap.

Bend over and try to touch your toes. No one looks good from this angle. Even if you have a six-pack, your skin will roll over your pants. Those of us without the six-pack have a little more that rolls over, but that only makes the picture more vivid. Your chin will sag to your chest. The bags under your eyes will swell as the blood rushes to your head. Your nose will have a direct line to your crotch.

And you wonder why you're miserable?

We weren't created to live bent over. We were created to live standing tall. But instead, we stay down, face in the ground, dreaming about this thing they call freedom. And we wonder why there's no peace and joy. Where's that abundant life Jesus promised?

Sweet one, it's here. It's free. You need only look up.

Jacob was a man who knew well the journey to freedom. He entered the world white-knuckled and tight-fisted, clutching his older brother's foot on his way out of the womb.[7] For his entire life, Jacob strived and fought for attention. He was a master at manipulation. He pretended to be his older brother in order to steal the birthright.[8] This grandson of Abraham had absolutely no idea who he was, but he struggled and strived to convince himself and everyone around him that he was worth something. Everything about his life was a game to get ahead and feed his ego.

In Genesis 32, we find him at the end of his rope. He's run away from one problem, only to run straight into another. Word comes that his older brother is just ahead, and Jacob flips. He's scared out of his mind, knees shaking, heart racing and mind swirling. The man he stole everything from is on his way with an army of 400. This day couldn't get any worse. It's like jumping out of the thistles right into the thorns.

So what did Jacob do? He did what he'd always done — fought for control. But this time, he fought God. Tight-fisted, he wrestled God in the dead of night. God was stronger, but Jacob wouldn't let go. Wouldn't let go of his plans for his life. Wouldn't let go of his bitterness. Wouldn't let go of every-thing he thought he deserved but never earned.

And God let him wrestle. He let him beat against His chest, knowing that Jacob's life hadn't been fair. Knowing that Jacob just needed to be held. And He would be there when Jacob finally let go.

Then He touched Jacob's hip socket and said, "Let go."[9] But even with a hip wrenched from its socket, Jacob wouldn't let go. He held on, eyes hard and unrelenting.

Through bated breath, he groaned, "I won't let go unless You bless me."

Oh, Jacob.

He was so desperate for worth. He was spinning, trying to spin the straw in his heart into gold.

Oh, Jacob. You are worth so much more than a couple of dollars.

And God whispered close, "What's your name?"[10]

God knew his name. It wasn't for God's benefit that He asked. He wanted Jacob to own it. Like Hagar in the desert, He wanted Jacob to look back on where he'd been. Like me in the closet, He was asking, *Who are you, sweet child of Mine?*

And Jacob called himself by name. Jacob. Deceiver. One who takes the place of another.[11]

There it is. Out in the open. Dirty laundry hanging on the line. Closet door busted open.

This is who I am, God. I'm a deceiver. I've tricked my way through life, pre-tending to be something I'm not. I'm broken and battered. I'm not enough, and no matter how hard I try, I never measure up.

With mask laid down and heart laid bare, Jacob placed his false identity at the altar. And God peeled back the layers of pretense, the masquerades, the disappointments, the fear and the shame. And there beneath the spot-light of stars shining bright against the velvet sky, the real Jacob stepped forward.

This is who I am, God. This is me. Deceiver. Trickster. Worthless.

And that Rescuer of hearts spoke like a bolt of sunlight straight through the darkness.

NOT ANYMORE!

That's not who you are anymore, Jacob. I'm giving you a new name — a new identity. From this moment on, you are no longer who you were. You've been made new.

God gave His child a new name — Israel, which means "God prevails, God perseveres, God fights."[12]

Jacob's old name had everything to do with Jacob. His character, his mistakes and his failures.

His new name had everything to do with God. God's character, God's power and what God wanted to do in Jacob's heart.

Can you picture yourself there in Jacob's story? Holding on tight-fisted to your dreams? Wrestling under God's hand there in the darkness? Pretending to be someone you're not?

What's your name, luv? Whatcha been calling yourself these days? Failure? Hopeless? Broken? Afraid? Rejected? Unusable? Unlovable? Unforgiveable? Unseen?

NOT ANYMORE!

Want to hear your new name, sweet daughter of the King? I'll let Him tell you …

"You'll get a brand-new name, straight from the mouth of God. You'll be a stunning crown in the palm of God's hand, a jeweled gold cup held high in the hand of your God. No more will anyone call you Rejected, and your country will no more be called Ruined. You'll be called My Delight … Because God delights in you."[13]

Do you realize that God delights in you? Do you believe it? What if that was how you lived? Believing that you are God's delight? What if you actually believed that was your name? The name you called yourself.

That old name is all about you, your mistakes and your failures.

Your new name is about God. His character, His power and what He wants to do in your heart.

He's made you new, sweet one. He calls you by a new name. But it's your choice what name you call yourself. You've been given a new name.

But first you need to own your false identity.

I realized I had called myself broken for so long that I believed it. My heart was broken so many times, but it never healed right. Like a bone that heals bent because it isn't set right, I thought I was too broken to be used by God. I thought I was too broken to find healing. I thought my marriage was too broken to do anything other than survive.

And as long as I believe that this is true, then it will be true.

Unless I stand up and say, "NOT ANYMORE!"

When we let go of our white-knuckled grip on our expectations of God and ourselves, transformation begins.

Transformation happens there in the darkness when we believe God is who He says He is and we are who He says we are. When the Word of God rings louder than the word of the snake, we stand up, with shaking knees at first, and life is never the same again.

Who doesn't long to be transformed? Free from the bondage of sin. Free from our insecurities, our shame, our fears. The Bible doesn't say transformation happens by trying harder. It doesn't say transformation occurs by feeling bad about ourselves and promising to do better next time.

How many of your promises to overcome sin have ever been fulfilled? Has focusing on your sin ever set you free?

Freedom is never found in promises to do better. Freedom is only found in discovering our identity in Christ.

The Bible tells us to *be transformed by the renewing of your mind.*[14]

Women ask me all the time, "What's my part?" They simply can't believe that it's as simple as this. Surely I must do something in order to change. Surely I can't simply be still and expect God to transform me.

What's your part? *Renew your mind. Exchange the lies with the truth.* It's claiming the truth of who you are as God changes you into who He already sees when He looks at you.

Brennan Manning writes, "The prayer of simple awareness means that we don't have to get anywhere because we are already there. We are simply coming into consciousness that we possess what we seek. Contemplation, defined as looking at Jesus while loving Him, leads not only to intimacy but to the transformation of the person contemplating."[15]

What lies are you believing about yourself today?

For many of us, there are lies that span across our entire lives — our identities are so wrapped up in them, we don't even know who we are without them. That snake tells me I'm too broken to be used by God. He tells me I'm too broken to find healing. He tells me my marriage is too broken to be fixed. What does it look like to put on the Spanx of truth?

My screen saver on my phone says this in bold letters: **You are not too broken.**

I'm going to look at it a hundred times a day until I believe it.

What lie do you need to exchange with truth? It's not enough to simply acknowledge the lie. It must be replaced with truth. Again and again and again — until you believe it. That's what putting on the Spanx of truth looks like. You pull them up so that when the battle is over, you'll still be standing!

When the enemy tells you God is disappointed in you, renew your mind.
God delights in you.[16]
When sin knocks at the door, renew your mind.
You've been set free.[17]
When jealousy takes hold of your heart, renew your mind.
You are a new creation.[18]
When self-pity makes itself at home, renew your mind.
The King of kings rejoices over you with singing.[19]
When you fail, renew your mind.

You are more than a conqueror.[20]
When you're scared, renew your mind.
The God of Heaven's armies is fighting on your behalf.[21]
When you believe you're not good enough, renew your mind.
You are chosen, holy, beloved, treasured, precious, righteous, forgiven and redeemed.[22]

Don't take my word for it. Look up these verses in the back of the book. Write them on your mirror. Hang them in your car. Tape them to your bed. Put on your Spanx of truth, girl! Get 'em on and keep 'em on!

In the battle for hearts, truth wins.

Every. Single. Time.

A little blond-haired, blue-eyed girl throws a tantrum on the kitchen floor because she believes nobody loves her.

A worn out, overwhelmed mama throws a temper tantrum on the bathroom floor because she believes she's too broken to stand tall.

And that snake has a party on our backs, because there on the floor, with dust mites and old Cheerios for companions, we stay small.

But I don't want to stay small. My babies need a mama who stands tall. So, I'm going to shake off that dust, put my Spanx on and live free.

There is truth. His name is Jesus. There is freedom. I've been set free. There is hope. He calls me Beloved. And there's a little girl out there, with eyes like sapphires, who needs the same truth that will set her free.

Because in the battle for hearts, truth wins.

The truth. The whole truth. And nothing but the truth. Oh, help us, God!

Every. Single. Time.

Digging Deeper

1. In what ways do you expect God to perform for you?

2. How can you put on the Spanx of truth this week regarding God's character?

3. What name have you been calling yourself lately?

4. Ask God what new name you need to claim as your identity.

5. How can you put on the Spanx of truth this week regarding your identity in Christ?

6. What does renewing your mind look like on a daily basis?

Chapter 9
Feathers for Your Nest

The spring air gusts fresh through the windows. A mama dove flutters back and forth from the trees to the trellis beside my front door. She's been busy all day, flittering to and fro, an urgency in her wings.

She's building, twig by twig, a nest to hold her babies. A refuge from the storm. A fortress from their foes. The daddy bird works beside her, hour after hour — their wings beating together with a common purpose. The time is short.

They rest for a moment on the roof, a secret conversation shared. I don't know what they are saying, but I can feel their excitement. I can sense their urgency.

Hurry up, mama! They're coming! I join in their song.

When the kids get home from school, I show them — finger to my lips. It's as if we're all in on a great secret, afraid that one wrong sound will blow our cover. One wrong move and the secret will get out. She looks at us, unsure of our intentions, but never losing her resolve. The blue around her eyes reminds me of the sky, and the look within her eyes reminds me of my heart.

I know, sweet mama. I know the days are long. I know, sweet mama. I know the days are hard. But it's worth it. I promise.

For three days, this mama bird works tirelessly on her nest. We watch, breath held tight, as she creates her home, all of us nearly bursting with excitement.

There's no more time. Weighed heavy with life, the mama bird nestles down in her home. The work is finished and yet only beginning. We get a chair to gain a better view.

And it's the ugliest nest I've ever seen in my life.

Three days building, and most of the twigs are on the ground. Three days creating, and we wonder if she's ever built a nest before. But as we each take a look, necks stretched, we gasp in awe. Two eggs lay beneath our mama dove. She cocks her head, never moving as we draw close. She's proud of her nest.

And I laugh to myself when I think about the irony of it.

This nest, far from perfect and far from beautiful, takes our breath away. And she isn't the slightest bit worried about any other nest but hers. There isn't another nest around to compare hers with. She sees her nest alone — this labor of love. And not one of us doubts her love. The kids climb higher to get a better look. Sturdy shoulders raise them up to catch a glimpse.

And we all sigh for the beauty of it.

She's been sitting there for a week now. Through the heat of the day. Through the storm in the night. Yet, still she sits, life growing safe beneath her. There in the darkness of her eggs, the mystery of transformation unfolds. I water the roses, and I look up into those eyes black as night. She looks back into mine, and we share a knowing glance.

The days are long, but oh, how quickly they go by.

A scream from the kitchen floats out the window, and she looks over, wondering at the source. I sigh. *Yes, mama. Those are my babies. Yes, I know they're loud.* Her eyes flick back to me, and I laugh.

I know it seems like you'll be up there on that nest forever, sweet mama. I know you wonder if this is ever going to end. It will, and it will be okay. They will be loud. They will drive you crazy. It will be hard. But they will be yours. And it will be worth it.

I turn off the hose, walk through the front door into my nest.

The kids are fighting — again.

The toilet is overflowing — again.

The kitchen is a mess — again.

The mystery of transformation is unfolding within these walls, and some days it feels like it will never end. But I know how quickly the days go by. And these are my chicks. This is my nest. And it's going to be okay.

The days are hard, but I know it's worth it.

I think about our mama bird perched on her nest. I can't wait to see those babies. Google says it takes two weeks for them to hatch, then two more weeks until they fly away. And there's a part of me that feels jealous of that mama by my front door. Four weeks of motherhood?

Maybe motherhood really is for the birds.

They say our time with our kids is short. We'll blink, and then they will be grown up and gone. We should be soaking up every second because all too soon the seconds turn into minutes, then turn into days and weeks and months and years.

And then they're gone.

I remember the trips to Walmart with three kids under the age of 4. Just trying to keep everyone alive every day took every ounce of my energy. We didn't have enough money to pay our bills, so organic food wasn't on the shopping list, let alone worrying about GMOs in the crackers. With one kid climbing up the shelves, another running down the aisles and another screaming in the cart, I wasn't thinking about making a lasting impact on their hearts.

I was thinking about crawling into a hole and disappearing.

I was also convinced that every person in the store was watching my meager attempts at mothering and came to the same conclusion as I — *what a joke — leave the mothering up to those of us who know what we're doing.*

Then those little old ladies, with their bright pink lipstick and wisdom-streaked hair, would smile at my little ones and say, "Enjoy it; it goes by so fast," as they patted me on the back and walked away.

And the only thing I could think was … *not fast enough!*

Yet deep down, I knew. I knew it would go fast. I wanted to enjoy it. But that day I was just trying to survive it. We all know the days go by quickly.

We all know we're supposed to enjoy every moment with our precious little chicks.

But how do we enjoy this short time when it feels like it's never going to end?

I tried enjoying it. Believe me, I did. I wanted nothing more than to love every second with those little house-destroying gremlins. But more often than not, I ended up on the bathroom floor, chocolate chips ground into the carpet, with everyone crying in timeout.

I stopped doing the dishes and played games all day, but then I ran around like a naked toddler on a sugar high because the dish fairy didn't show up. I read the books and blogs. They told me to enjoy it. They told me all my children needed was me.

All. Day. Long.

So I gave them me.

All. Day. Long.

And nobody seemed to be enjoying anything. Is motherhood meant to look like our mama dove, sitting in my nest day after day? Maybe. But is there more to motherhood?

Is it more than simply getting through the day? I knew I was supposed to enjoy it. But how? Most days I just wanted to fly the coop. And then I felt guilty for not enjoying it.

How do we enjoy the moments when the days feel like eternity?

I wanted to be a good mom.

I tried to be a good mom.

I failed at being a good mom.

And then I discovered mother ducks.

Mother ducks are good moms.

Like other birds, they build nests for their little ones, a refuge from the storm and fortress from their foes. But unlike other birds, mother ducks build their nests with feathers plucked from their own breasts.[1] With their beaks, they pull feathers from their chests to line their nests. These feathers make their nests soft — make them safe. A sanctuary sewn with the down of a mother's heart. A home hewn with the offering of a mother's life.

It costs mother ducks something to be a mom. There are always feathers lying on the ground — feathers fallen from the running around and daily squirmishes. But they don't use those feathers. They don't take from the leftovers. They give the best of themselves to their children. It's a sacrifice — one they freely give.

This sounds beautiful, doesn't it? When I first heard about this, I immediately wanted to be like a mother duck. I realized I was giving my children my leftovers. Taking home-cooked dinners to others while my kids ate mac and cheese. Poor babies. Those days when success meant keeping everyone alive, I clearly wasn't sacrificing enough. I wasn't giving enough. I needed to give them everything in order to be a good mom.

So I began plucking feathers like nobody's business. Every second. Every heartbeat. Every opportunity. Every blog that told me to do something with my children, I did it. Every article that said, "The time is short. Make the most of it!" weighed heavily on my heart as I realized I wasn't doing enough. I had to give more. I had to be more. If I loved them, that's what I would do, right?

Who needs clean underwear when there are games to be played? Who needs clean dishes when there are hearts to be molded?

Isn't that motherhood, this giving of our feathers so our little ones feel safe, loved and valued?

But then a thought struck me.

In my whole life long, I've never seen a naked duck running around.

And when I thought about it, I couldn't think of anything uglier than a naked duck running around.

Imagine it with me for a moment. Have you ever seen a mother duck without any feathers? That's because there are no naked ducks running around out there. They don't pluck all of their feathers.

Yes, it costs them something. It's a sacrifice to pull a feather out of their chest. But they don't pull them all. They pluck just enough to make their nests soft — to make their nests safe. No, they don't take from the leftovers lying on the ground. They also don't take the feathers from another mama duck's nest. They give of themselves with feathers plucked from their own breasts — their own hearts.

And when I looked at all the mamas around me, building nests for their children — trying to be everything in every way — I realized there were a lot of naked ducks running around.

Yes, motherhood costs something. It costs a lot, actually. Like flat tummies and bladders that don't leak. Like sleep and sanity ... and vaginas that aren't ripped and scarred. But how many of us think we must give everything, until there's nothing left? How many of us are looking around at everyone else, worried that if we don't give what she's giving, it means we must not love our children?

That's the beauty of this picture. Your feathers are not my feathers. Yes, my feathers will cost me something. But I don't have to come over to your nest and take yours. I can give from my heart and let you give from yours.

This concept transformed my view of motherhood. I realized that God made me unique as a mom, with feathers in my own heart to give my children. Yes, there are days when I give the leftovers. When the living of this life gets in the way, and we simply make it through the day. But I spent so many years looking at everyone else, thinking that I needed to measure up to them, that I missed how freeing it was to simply be myself with my kids.

Baking cookies with small children is not one of my feathers. *Gasp!* I know you're surprised. So I stopped. Now that my kids are older, we do bake cookies together from time to time. But only with one kid at a time.

Sewing my children's clothes is not one of my feathers. Don't want it. Don't need it.

Reading books is one of my feathers. I love literature. I love stories. So I give that part of my heart to my kids. We spend hours reading. When my kids were younger, before sports and activities filled our evenings, I read to my kids individually every night. Ryan traveled for work, so bedtime fell on me every night during the week. It took me two hours to put my kids to bed each night. And I loved every second of it. Selah and I read *The Secret Garden* together, and through it, we found a common ground that brought us closer together.

No one was crying — except for at the end when Collin runs into his daddy's arms — but who doesn't cry at that? No one was in timeout, and I actually enjoyed the time with my kids.

For the first time as a mom, my nest felt soft. It felt safe. Why? Because I wasn't trying to be anyone other than myself.

We've read more books together than I can count. And the time has been sweet. My children will remember those nights, snuggled up together. And maybe those memories will outshine the times when we tried baking cookies.

Am I telling you to spend two hours putting your kids to bed at night? Absolutely not. Unless you want to. Unless that is one of your feathers. I had two hours at night to be with my kids because I wasn't spending my days baking cookies and sewing their clothes.

But reading two hours every night doesn't make you a good mom.

We have to redefine what makes a good mom. We have to redefine success as a mom. As long as we're looking at everyone else, measuring our success next to someone else, we'll always come up short. Or we'll be running around like a bunch of naked ducks. And no earthly Spanx can make that look good.

My youngest child didn't like reading big books with me, so I had to find different feathers for her. But she loves to play games. And she loves to go on walks. So, that's what we do. And the time is sweet.

I play catch with my son, and we camp as a family. I've let Ryan find his feathers, as well. He loves to cook with those children. And he's learned from experience that the dish fairy doesn't exist. He loves to take them to the grocery store and let all of them pick out the food. And he's learned from experience that bruised apples don't taste good.

What feathers are you lining your nest with? It's okay to simply survive some days. If your kids are under the age of 3, then most days you will simply survive. But I believe motherhood is more than just making it through the day.

You have been created, sweet mama, with a beautiful, unique heart. What feathers can you pull from your heart to line your nest? And how many feathers in your nest are actually someone else's?

Let's go back and talk about that standard you're trying to meet as a mom. How much of it stems from someone else? It's great to read good books and learn from other moms. But if you walk away feeling guilty, then maybe that's not one of your feathers. And maybe that's okay. They say the time is short. It is. They say to enjoy the moments. We should. But if your moments are spent feeling guilty, then you're not enjoying anything.

I realized that a lot of my standards for motherhood came from watching my mom. She was the party queen. She ran fundraisers for our school. She transformed our house for every holiday. As God peeled away the layers of guilt around my heart, I had to look through them to see which feathers I was taking from someone else and which feathers were my own.

I love parties. So I throw birthday bashes for my kids. And I love every second of it. I spend weeks preparing for their birthday parties. Ryan asked me one time if Emery was getting married or turning 3. I said, "Either way, you gotta make those cucumber sandwiches, babe."

I learned that I don't need to run the fundraisers at my kids' school. I love to decorate. I hate sewing. I love hiking. I hate swimming. For the love of all that is good, this hair and chlorine do not mix, children!

Now, before you get your feathers all in a bunch, I'm not saying that I will never do anything I don't like doing simply because I don't have to. I don't love Monopoly, but by golly, I will still play it because my son wants me to. But this has given me the ability to filter my days and lay aside my guilt. When I see the success of a friend and feel the guilt inching in, I can look back on my week and say, "Remember how you laughed with your kids as you read *The Tale of Desperaux* together? Remember that game of H-O-R-S-E you played the other day? Remember that bike ride as you chased the sun down the horizon?"

I put on my Spanx of truth, and the guilt slides off. Guilt does that when we stand tall. When my friends post pictures of their holiday traditions, I can remind myself of the memories I made with my kids when we traipsed through the forest last summer. My children's memories will not be your children's memories. And that's okay.

What are your feathers? What are the unique things about you that you can pull from your chest to give your children? If you want to make your own baby food, then you go for it, girl! But if you're doing it because you think you're supposed to, then don't! If sewing your kids' clothes is one of your feathers, then I commend you! If it's not, then spend your time elsewhere. If baking cookies with those little people fills you with joy, then bake the freaking cookies! If you love decorating your house, then do it.

Stop feeling guilty for what you're not doing, and stop making someone else feel guilty for not being you.

That's the beauty of knowing who we are in Christ and who we are uniquely as moms. We don't have to push someone else down in order to make ourselves feel tall. We can each be who we're called to be.

Making the most of the time doesn't mean we have to make every second count. Making the most of the time means choosing which moments to make count. Sometimes it means our kids watch Netflix all day while we read the *Twilight* books (I'm talking about someone else, of course). Sometimes it means we spend the whole day playing games with our little loves. And sometimes it means we clean the house while the kids stare bored through the back door. Sometimes it means we spend hours reading under blankets. And sometimes it means *you kids better get your booties outta this house and play outside so mama doesn't lose her mind!* Sometimes it means watching clouds roll by on the trampoline. And sometimes it means watching the clouds roll by from a lawn chair with a margarita in hand. Sometimes it means holding little faces in our hands, kissing cheeks and tickling chins. And sometimes it means *get your cute little face out of mine so I can drink my margarita in peace!*

What if we gave each other freedom to be ourselves? What if one mom's success didn't make the rest of us feel like failures? What if we each embraced our own unique calling as moms and empowered each other to do the same? If loving your kids looks like Easter crafts from Pinterest and baking bread from scratch, and loving my kids looks like planting veggies in the garden and bike rides on summer nights, then let's tell each other good job and get back to the living of this life with our faces lifted up to the sky!

Let's start a movement, shall we? Let's start the "no more naked ducks" movement. It begins with us. You and me. I decide that my feathers are enough for my children, and you decide that your feathers are enough for your children. You don't have to steal mine, and I don't have to steal yours. And neither of us is worried about if one is better than the other. Only then will our nests become soft — and safe. A refuge from the storm. A fortress from our foes.

Because we all know that the time is short. And our enemy knows it, too.

Is there ever a place we need the Spanx of truth more than in motherhood? In the battle for hearts, truth wins. Every. Single. Time.

In your home, truth wins.

In your marriage, truth wins.

With your children, truth wins.

But we must know the truth in order for the truth to set us free.

The Truth About Motherhood

What is the point of motherhood?

I'm sure you've asked this question when your house looks like crap and your kids are fighting for the umpteenth time today. But what is the point?

Is it to make us feel good about ourselves?

Is it to prove to the world that we're true women, capable of all feminine expectations?

Is it to raise intelligent, responsible citizens who help society?

Is it to raise kids who know a lot of Bible verses, use good manners and someday overcome all of their annoying habits?

Is it to keep everyone alive one day after another?

Have you ever asked this question — besides when you're curled up on the bathroom floor while children resembling Frankenstein's offspring poke little hands under the door?

So what's the point? What are we doing all of this for? Is it to give our kids a magical childhood without any disappointment, fear or pain? Is it to win the supermom award when our kids say the real meaning of Christmas to the grocery store clerk?

Whatever your point is for motherhood will determine your steps in getting there.

Yes, let's keep our children alive. But let's do more than that. Let's figure out who we are in Christ, live standing tall and teach our children to do the same.

If the snake uses the same ploy with me that he used with Jesus, then you can bet he's after my kids. If he has gone to so much trouble to keep my face down in the dust, then I have two goals as a mom.

1. Tell my kids who God is.
2. Tell my kids who they are.

Oh, and get them to stop eating with their mouths open. Seriously.

That snake is after me. He's after my husband. He's after my kids. And there is no way in Hell I'm just gonna stay looking at the ground, letting him have a party on my back. There's no way I'm going to live bent over anymore, worried about how I compare to Susie down the street or Debbie across the table.

It's time to stand up, mama! It's time to shake off that snake, stand up tall and shout truth over our children.

Take the word failure out of your vocabulary. Your identity is not tied to your failures. Your identity is not tied to your performance. So let's stop wasting time staring at our toes and start looking up into the eyes of grace.

Let's stop fighting each other, and let's start fighting that snake.

He wants our kids to believe that God is not good and they are not loved. If he can get them to believe that God is holding out on them and they are not enough, then the cycle continues. The next generation of mamas will continue performing and comparing — naked mama ducks with their heads in the dust.

My goal as a mom is not to win the supermom award anymore.

My goal is not to outperform my friends.

My goal is not to raise well-behaved children.

My goal is not to find fulfillment in my children.

My goal is to tell them that they are loved by a good God. And they can live standing tall. This has become my mantra as a mom. I whisper it to my children as I turn off the light.

Sweet babies, God is good. And you are loved.

I talk about it on the way to school.

Little ones, God is strong. And you are redeemed.

I speak over them as I fix their hair.

Child of the King, God is faithful. And you are enough.

I tell them when they've made a mistake.

Precious one, that is not who you are. You are a new creation. And you have been made new.

And I'm going to keep saying it until the truth rings louder than the lies in their little hearts. And when mamas and their children rise up in truth, we can change the world.

In the same way that I strive for worth in the applause of the crowd, so my children strive for worth in the approval of their peers. In the same way I long for more when I don't believe God is enough, so my children yearn for something to satisfy the hollow space in their hearts.

Behavior is almost always tied to worth. They fight because they want to be seen. They talk back because they want to be heard. They lie because they're scared to death they're not enough. And they strive and struggle, searching for worth in all the wrong places, because that snake wants them to believe that their God is not good, and they are not loved.

What if my children don't have to live bent over? What if they believe God is good and they are loved right now? What if they walk out of our home each morning confident in who God is and who they are in Him instead of worrying about making me look good by their behavior? What if I stop wondering if I did enough to prove to the world I'm a good mom and focus instead on giving my children the truth that sets them free?

The world is harsh. The enemy is real. Now that my kids are older, the stakes are higher. We're entering the teenage years, and let me tell you, baking cookies is not the goal anymore.

Calling out my children's true identity as children of God is.

And if I can do that while we bake cookies, then bring on the mess!

When I focus more on *my* nest and my feathers, and less about proving that I'm a good mom, then I am free to be the mom God made me to be for *my* children.

I am the perfect mom for my kids — not yours. But I don't have to be perfect in order to be the mom they need.

I can just be me.

And when I let myself be me, then I let my children be themselves, too. And a home where no one needs to perform is a home that is safe indeed.

When did we start believing the lie that our children's behavior gives us worth? When did we decide that comparing them to other children somehow makes us better? I am not raising robots. I am not raising good citizens. I am raising image bearers of the King of kings.

Are the stakes high? You betcha.

Do the moments count? Oh, yes, they do.

Then why am I wasting moments worried about how my kids measure up to yours? The stakes are too high. The time is too short. Let's put our measuring sticks away and let our kids be who God made them to be.

When I lay down my expectations of my children, and instead lead them to the heart of Jesus, then mom-wins and mom-fails aren't how I measure success. I become less concerned with being a good mom. Because, when God calls my children by name, and they press their ears against His chest, hearing His heart beating for them, then that's a God-win. And He's a good God.

Imagine what God will do through my kids if they march confidently into this world, standing tall and free.

Peer pressure? Not interested.

Popularity? Don't need it.

Applause? Approval? Fitting in? I've already got all I need in *Him*.

Because in the battle for hearts, truth wins. Every. Single. Time.

The Truth About Other Moms

Do you remember our friend Jacob? So desperate for worth. Holding so tight to what he thought his life should look like. He still had to face Esau. We didn't get to that part of the story.

Esau was coming for Jacob with an army of 400 men.[2] That's enough to make you wet your pants no matter how many Kegels you do at stoplights.

Once upon a time, Jacob had stolen everything from Esau, his insecurity forging its mark through an entire family. Insecurity, weaving a trail of brokenness in its wake, followed Jacob everywhere he went. And eventually, it led him right back into his brother's hands.

But that night, everything changed.

Jacob met the real God. Not just the God of his ancestors. Not just the God of Isaac and Abraham. Up to this point, Jacob referred to God as the God of his fathers. When he prayed, he said, "God of Isaac. God of Abraham."[3]

God wasn't *his* God yet. It wasn't *his* story yet.

Then he met God for himself, and he was forever changed. Given a new name. A name that tells the story of God's redemptive work that could heal this family and make broken things new.

That's what happens when we realize who we are in Christ. The sin weaved through generations can stop. Broken hearts are made new. And a new story of redemption flows down through the pages of our stories.

Esau was Jacob's enemy, and Esau had every right to be angry. But as they faced each other, Jacob didn't see his enemy. Instead, he saw a friend. Esau didn't come to fight. He came to restore. Esau didn't come for revenge. He came to forgive.

There with knees trembling and heart thrashing, Jacob experienced the reckless, scandalous, unmerited, untamed, incomprehensible wonder of grace. And he beheld it in the face of his brother. Esau ran to Jacob, threw his arms around him — and they wept together over the lost years.

Through sobs of joy, Jacob said, "Seeing your face is like seeing the face of God."[4]

I don't know what happened to Esau in the years between his stolen birthright and this moment. But his choice to lay down his sword and instead reach out his arms to his brother changed everything.

He of all people knew Jacob's mistakes. He knew the old Jacob — and he loved him, anyway.

God must have done something in Esau's heart in those years.

Instead of giving Jacob what he deserved, he extended God's grace, and Jacob finally saw the truth.

When we know who we are in Christ, we see each other from a different perspective. When we lay down our measuring sticks and show up with nothing to prove to each other, we realize that in each other is where we see God most.

In your face, I see God at work in my life. In my eyes, you see God's love for you.

Jacob then named the place they were standing El-Elohe-Israel.[5] Guess what that means? God — the God of Israel. Remember Jacob's new name? Israel. God is now *his* God. This is *his* story now. Not just the story of his father and grandfather. When he saw the face of God in his brother, he knew that he really could let go — of the measuring, the fighting, the spinning and the striving. He wasn't alone.

And a new thread weaved through the family line — the thread of grace.

It's one thing to hear God loves you. You might even believe it. But to see His love for you in the face of someone else, that's when it becomes real.

Maybe the reason we all struggle so much to believe that God really loves us is because we don't see it in each other's faces. We see judgement when we look at each other instead of grace. And maybe that's why the world can't believe it, either.

We weren't made to do this thing alone, sweet mama. We need each other. We need to lay down our measuring sticks and start being the ones who speak truth into each other's lives. We need to stop being the ones who push each other down and become the ones who build each other up. We have the opportunity to be the face of God to each other. So that God's love isn't something we've heard about, but something we've actually seen with our own two eyes.

We're all longing for it, aren't we? That's why we keep showing up at the places women gather. We're hoping for a glimpse of our Jesus in each other.

Sarah Bessey invites us to lay down our swords as we do this thing called life together. She reminds us that "we are seeking Jesus — we want to smell Him on the skin of others, and we want to hear tell of His activity. We are seeking fellow travelers for the journey. We are hungry for a community, a place to tell our stories and to listen, to love well, to learn how to have eyes to see and ears to hear. We want to be part of something amazing and real and lasting, something bigger than ourselves. We want to be with other women who know and love and follow our Jesus. Somehow we know that we will love Him better if we hear from others how much they love Him, too."[6]

Your highest calling is not motherhood. Your highest calling is the privilege of bearing the image of God.

He is in you, sweet one, if you have called upon His name. Now you get to be His face to others.

Yes, motherhood is sacred. It's hard. And it's oh so very important. But you were made first in the image of God. And because of God's impossible grace, He makes broken things new. And now, in you, He reveals Himself to the world.

I've heard people say that it's not about us. They say the relationship we have with this cross-bearing God is about His glory and not about us. I think they're afraid we might get big heads and forget how lowly and unforgiveable we really are. But why would God have sacrificed His only Son to be with us if it isn't about us? "We give glory to God simply by being ourselves."[7] Our true selves. Not the women we're trying to turn ourselves into, but the women God sees when He looks at us. We can only live as our true selves if we see ourselves the way God sees us. Not as unforgiveable. But forgiven, through and through.

It doesn't end with us, though. God chooses to use us to reveal His love story to this world. To the mama across the table. To the mama down the street. To the children in your home.

This doesn't happen by becoming smaller.

It happens when we remember who God is and who we are in Him.

You are loved by a good God. And so is that mama you're comparing yourself to. Go tell her she has a beautiful nest. Go tell her what she's doing matters. Tell her that she matters.

Go be the face of God to a mama who's lost her way in the darkness.

Together, we can change this world. But not until we put our measuring sticks down.

They say the time is short. It is.

They say we should enjoy it. We should. And I think we can.

You with your feathers, and I with mine. Like our mama dove, proud of what we've built because it's ours. This is my nest. These are my chicks. And it's so very worth it.

Most days I don't have a clue what I'm doing. But I love those little people. And for some wild reason, they love me back.

I know the days are long, sweet mama. I know the days are hard. These days of nest building can leave a heart tattered and worn. My nest won't look like yours, and that's okay. But when you come over to mine for a cup of tea, may you find a refuge from the storm and a fortress from your foes. Not because my nest is perfect. But because my love is evident.

When we show up with nothing to prove, fully loved by a good God, then we won't see each other as the enemy any longer.

Instead, we'll lift each other's faces up out of the dust. And we'll all sigh for the beauty of it.

Digging Deeper

1. Have you ever felt like a naked duck running around?

2. In what areas are you plucking too many feathers?

3. In what areas are you plucking too few feathers — giving the leftovers?

4. In what ways are you stealing feathers from other mamas?

5. What are your unique feathers you can line your nest with?

6. What is the point of motherhood for you? How are you getting there?

7. Who has been "the face of God" to you?

8. Who do you need to forgive or stop comparing yourself to in order to be the face of God to that person?

Chapter 10
What If ...?

I am awakened from the depths of night with the quiet beckoning of an unseen whisper.

Come and see something, He murmurs softly in my ear — that Voice I recognize but so rarely heed.

"Oh, but my bed is so warm. My eyes are so heavy. The darkness is so cozy," I answer back.

Yet deep in my heart I know that if I don't get up, I will miss something.

How many miracles have I missed simply because I wasn't watching? How many discoveries have I overshadowed with my excuses? How many glimpses of Heaven have I exchanged for the promise of comfort?

My body is tired and craves sleep, but my soul is exhausted and longs for freedom.

The whisper grows louder. *Come and see something, child. Come and be with Me.*

So I rise, tired, stumbling — afraid. The weight of yesterday's mistakes grips my shoulders, pressing down hard upon my heart. I prepare my repentance speech, as if I'm tiptoeing to the Throne, head hung low. Afraid that what He'll see when I arrive will cause Him to change His mind — turn His head in disapproval.

The stillness of night envelops me as I sit bundled in an embrace of wool, my eyes slowly awakening to the coming grandeur. I look toward the east, awaiting that indescribable moment when light bursts forth and darkness scurries to hide.

The trees grow silent in anticipation. The sunflowers bow before the unseen Presence. My breath catches as the flames of morning lick the horizon and the earth erupts into song. Their song seeps into my soul, and I cannot help but join in their chorus. Here in the solitude of morning, basking in the blaze of fire, the scales on my eyes and the walls around my heart dissolve into the beauty.

I hear the whisper again.

I'm here. Do you see Me? I'm not only in the brilliance. I'm in the cries of your toddler.

I'm in the mounds of laundry hiding in your closets.

I'm in the brokenness of your dreams.

I'm in the hush of the evening.

I'm in your chaos, your laughter, your tears and ... yes, even in your darkness. You're safe here with Me.

"But, God, I'm so far from where I want to be. I've messed up too many times to count."

My child, remember who I am. Remember who you are.

Do you believe I'm big enough to carry that burden of yours?

Do you believe I'm big enough to satisfy your longings?

Do you believe you're loved enough to trust Me?

Do you believe I'm bigger than your fears?

Look up, child. Look up and remember.

I'm beginning to see. I'm learning to allow the holy access into every aspect of life. To allow my wounds to be wells of healing that can be poured out for others.

As I sit in the silence of morning, I look around and I see. I see Him all around me. Gifts poured out for His child — not because I've earned them — but because He's a lavish Father who loves to give good gifts. The weight of my guilt slips off as I stare into His face. As truth washes over me, I'm reminded that I don't have to try harder.

I don't have to tiptoe to the Throne.

I can run, limp, crawl — whatever it takes — straight into my Abba's arms.

Sweet mama, can you hear it? Is it getting louder against your ear? The thrum of your Abba's heart beating for you. The longer you listen, the louder it becomes. Until the lies become merely cries in the distance.

I know you're still not sure. That's okay. It takes time. I'll tell you again, though.

Your God is good. And you are loved.

The time has come, friend. It's time to get up and start living fully alive and fully awake. It's time to change our perspective. Of God, ourselves, our children and each other.

I know life hasn't turned out the way you expected. I know you love those kids. And I know those kids drive you crazy. But it's time to take the first step. The first step forward.

God is calling you on an adventure with Him. This thing called motherhood. It's hard. These days of nest building. They're long. But if you open your eyes, you'll see it. Right there in the midst of the hard, there are treasures. Right there in the darkness, God's goodness is passing by.

Are you watching?

Or are you still stuck in that pit of fear, insecurity and shame? It's okay, if you are. We're here to help. Your sisters — fellow pit dwellers. Put your foot in my hands. I'll hoist you up. I might have a kid clinging to my legs while we're at it, but I'm here.

Take my hand, and I'll pull you up.

We were created to live fully alive and fully awake. If you have a newborn, don't worry, we'll let you keep sleeping. Just for a little bit longer. But deep down, don't we all long for adventure? To live a life that changes the world?

Sadly, most of us never even make it out of the pit.

There's a man in the Bible who spent a good amount of time in a pit. We find him in Judges 6.

The Israelites were in desperate need of a miracle. It had been 300 years since they marched victoriously into the Promised Land. Things didn't turn out the way they planned, though, and now they were one step short of slavery to the Midianites.

Food was scarce. Hope was scarcer.

Where was the God of Abraham, Isaac and Jacob? Where was the God of Moses? Where were His wonders and promises?

These were the cries of God's people, burdened down by the weight of their past mistakes and current disappointments. Fear had become the norm in this world. Safety was paramount to survival.

And that's what they were doing — surviving.

But God heard their cries. He knew they needed a Savior, and He had a rescue plan up His sleeve.

At just the right time, God found Gideon hidden in a pit of hopelessness. No, literally, he was in a pit. In the ground. That's how bad things were.

Gideon was just a normal guy, going about his daily business of threshing the wheat. Down in a pit because he had to hide the wheat from the Midianites. There was nothing special about him. Nothing that would cause another to take a second look.

There in the mundane rhythm of life, God found him.

And because God couldn't stand to be apart from His children, He went looking for Gideon.

There in the pit, God called him by name. "Mighty hero, the Lord is with you!"[1]

"Who, me?" Gideon asks. "You must have the wrong guy. I'm just a wheat thresher. I'm just a nobody, here in a pit of fear and despair."

But he realized who he was talking to, and he started to get a bit irked. This was, after all, the God of Israel, right? Where was He now? Where was the God who brought down Jericho's walls? And then he pleaded his case.

Things were bad. Nothing was fair. "Why?" he implored. "Why has God let this happen to us? Where are all the miracles we've heard about? Where is this God who brought us out of Egypt? Clearly He isn't here, and if He is, then He must not care."[2]

And God listened. He let Gideon grieve over the life he thought he would have. He let Gideon weep over the broken dreams and unmet expectations.

Gideon was in the Promised Land. This was supposed to be the land flowing with milk and honey.

But happily-ever-after doesn't exist this side of Heaven, even in the Promised Land. And you can live in a pit, even in the Promised Land.

But then God answered, "Go with the strength you have, and rescue Israel from the Midianites. I am sending you!"[3]

"What? Not me. I'm from the weakest family, and I'm the weakest in my family! You've definitely got the wrong guy here. Me? A hero? Me? A rescuer? Not a chance."[4]

And the Lord responded, "I will be with you."[5]

This is the beauty of our God. He calls us by our new name before we ever live up to that name. God saw Gideon as a warrior. So He called Gideon a warrior. Gideon had a hard time believing it, though. His life didn't reflect this name. He'd been hiding in a pit, too afraid to step into the light. Too afraid of the danger to show his face. He hadn't done anything to deserve his new name.

But that's the point.

New names are about what God is going to do in us, not anything we've done for Him. We already have everything we need in Christ.

God told Gideon to "go with the strength you have."

How? Because the God of Heaven's army was going, too!

The same power that raised Christ from the dead lives in you, sweet mama.[6] Imagine the possibilities if we really believed it was true.

When Gideon finally believed he was the warrior God called him, his story took a turn. That's when he marched out of the mundane and into the adventure.

God is in the business of setting captives free. It starts with us. But it certainly doesn't end with us.

First, Gideon had to believe he was really who God said he was. He became a warrior because God saw him as a warrior. He didn't have to prove himself as a warrior first.

Why?

Because it was all about God's strength and God's presence. All Gideon had to do was show up with a new way of thinking. He already had all that he needed. He was enough, simply because God was enough.

Gideon also had to give up his ideas of who God should be in his life. God didn't show up the way Gideon thought He should. His timing didn't fit Gideon's timing. He wanted a miracle. And he wanted it yesterday.

God gave him a miracle. He gave the Israelites a miracle.

The miracle was Gideon — a normal guy set free in order to set the captives free.

Do you see it, sweet mama? God wants to use you and me. Right here in the mundane rhythm of life. That's the mystery of transformation unfolding in our lives. When you and I believe we don't have to live with our faces in the dust any longer, we stand up straight. And then we go tell others that they can stand up straight, too. Our children, our friends … on and on until the whole wide world knows.

You and I are the miracle. You and I are the answer to someone's prayers. When Gideon asked where God was, God answered … *in you, Gideon*.

When you sink into that pit of despair, wondering where God is in the midst of suffering. When the pain of this world threatens to squeeze the very breath out of your lungs, and you cry out, "Where are You, God?" His answer is the same … *in you, sweet mama*.

But we'll never do anything if we stay down there in that pit.

When you actually believe you are loved, then you are free to offer the same love you've been given to others. That snake has us fooled into believing that feeling too loved will make us too self-centered. Yes, if we are full of self-love.

But when we are loved completely by our good God, then we can't help but join in His purpose — loving a world lost in darkness and setting captives free. We are told to love our neighbor, and we all truly want to. I believe that. But we can't ever fully love until we know how loved we are.

Love your neighbor as yourself.[7] Well, if I don't like who I am, and I wonder how God would ever find me acceptable, then that's how I will love my neighbor. And the cycle goes on and on.

I can beat you over the head until I'm blue in the face telling you how you should give your money, time and love to this world. But rest against the heartbeat of Jesus long enough, and you won't need a hammer to the head. You'll be free to love because you have been loved.

And you won't be able to stop yourself.

When I talk about identity, people always caution me against too much grace. "We need a balance of grace and truth," they say.

Grace is truth, sweet one. And truth is grace. They are not separate. You cannot have one without the other.

"But if we focus too much on how much God loves us, then we'll become selfish and self-centered," they warn.

If you are leaning up against the chest of Jesus, listening to His heart beat for you, then it is only a matter of time before your heart will start to catch the rhythm. And the rhythm is this:

The heart of Jesus beats for you ... and it beats for others, too. If you are listening to the heart of your Abba, the One who moved Heaven and earth to rescue His children, then you cannot stay where you are for long. Your feet begin to move in step. Your hands begin to move with the beat. And suddenly you are calling to others, "Come over here! Come and see that the Lord is good! Come and taste His love!"[8]

You never need to fear being too loved. True love casts out fear. And when we stop living afraid, we start living free.

Picture a billionaire for a moment. He's a good and loving billionaire. He has everything at his disposal. There's a woman sitting outside the gate of his home. She sits in tattered clothes in the dust. Sadness echoes across her dirt-smeared face. She's starving. Lonely. Afraid. The billionaire comes to her at the gate, and he gives her a million dollars.

Can you imagine her joy? Can you imagine her gratitude? He tells her to use the money wisely. He tells her to give of it generously. She will forever be grateful to her savior, won't she? He changed her life. How could she not be grateful?

Now picture that same billionaire and that same woman. She's outside the gates — tattered clothes and dirt-smeared face. She comes, day after day, hoping for just a morsel to fill her aching belly. The billionaire looks her in the eye. He opens the gate and says, "My daughter, you're finally home. You're my child now. Everything I have is yours. Come and go freely. All of my resources are at your disposal. All of this is now yours. Your belly will never be empty. You'll never lack for anything. You are mine, and all I have is yours."

This is what happens when we realize who we are as daughters of the King.

We were not just given a million dollars. We were not just given a ticket out of Hell. We were adopted as daughters, and now the resources of the King are ours. We are inside the gates. And we are loved. And because we know the heart of our good and generous Father, we also give out of His abundance. We invite others in because there's room at the table for everyone.

Are you living as the recipient of an amazing gift, or are you living as an adopted child with full access to the gift-giver? It changes how we live.

When we stop living afraid, we start living free.

As moms, we know fear all too well, don't we? From the moment we hold our babies to our breasts, fear becomes a constant companion. I didn't know I would bring home two babies from the hospital. Two babies I would feed, nurture and watch grow from that day forward. But fear came tagging along.

I packed it in my bag, strapped it in the car and watched it grow bigger and bigger every day. Fear runs in my veins. And it feeds on insecurity.

How many nights have you lain awake, your list of *what ifs* running through your mind?

What if my kids get sick …?

What if my husband loses his job …?

What if my kids get kidnapped …?

What if there isn't enough money to pay the bills …?

What if there's a shooting at the school …?

What if there's a shooting at the church …?

The list goes on and on, doesn't it? What's your list? What keeps you awake at night?

What if my kids get hurt …?

What if they reject me …?

What if I fail …?

What if I'm not enough …?

What if I end up disappointed …?

What if God really isn't enough …?

Just like shame, fear is always rooted in a lie.

Remember that snake? He's trying to get you to believe that God is not good and you are not loved.

What lies are you believing right now that have made you afraid?

A couple years ago, Selah came home from school with news that sent my heart catapulting out my chest. A boy in her class called her a name I didn't know fourth-graders knew. The sheltered world I worked so tirelessly to construct for my family crumbled around me as I realized how little control I really had.

"He called you what?" I asked, gripping the counter as my heart plummeted into my stomach.

Surely I just misheard what she said. Surely a fourth-grader doesn't know about these things. But she said it again.

I looked up at Ryan, searching his face for answers. Searching his eyes for an anchor to grasp as my fears began to take me down.

For 20 agonizing minutes, I tried to ignore my racing, raging heart as I tucked the other kids into bed. Twenty minutes to find enough wisdom to speak truth into a 9-year-old's heart. And I realized I was bankrupt. I didn't have what it takes to be a parent in these perilous times. My fear was all I could see. And those fears were materializing into reality before my very eyes.

Those nights lying awake wondering, "What if?" were now becoming "What now?" And I fought the urge to sink into despair.

We sat down and started to talk. Questions I didn't want to ask. Answers I didn't want to hear. And yet a conversation unfolded that would ring in my heart as one of the most precious I have ever had. I caught a glimpse of her thoughts — thoughts she often keeps guarded. I snuck a peek at her heart — a heart she rarely leaves exposed.

We talked about things that are uncomfortable. And we laughed.

We talked about things that are scary. And we dreamed.

We replaced the secrets with light, the lies with truth and the fears with courage.

Light, truth and courage can only come from the One who fills my bankrupt soul to overflowing.

Yet my fears still lingered. So it wasn't as bad as I thought ... but "what if ...?"

My instincts told me, Run! Hide! Make sure that nothing bad ever happens so we can be safe.

I lay awake wrestling with my thoughts. That question still burning a hole in my mind.

"What if ...?"

"God, where are You?"

In you, sweet one.

As I remembered the truth, I began asking a different question. A question that sent my fears running.

"What if my kids fall so madly in love with Jesus, they flood their school with light?"

"What if my kids see a mom who knows who she is in Christ and stops comparing herself to others?"

"What if we stopped trying to live safe and began living free?"

And as my fears retreated into the shadows, I grew restless for a different reason.

My soul began to stir with excitement. My heart began to break for this boy, and for so many others who need someone to love them. Someone to share Jesus with them. After all, darkness is merely the absence of light. Darkness has no power of its own. It's only when the light stops shining that darkness reigns. It can't remain in the presence of light.

And I wondered, maybe instead of shaking our heads at the darkness of the world, what would happen if we began shining the light in it? Light shines on truth, and truth always sets us free. That's where I want to live.

That's where I choose to live.

It's always a choice, though. I can hide in my fear anytime I want. But that's not living.

Gideon wasn't truly living down in that pit. Yes, he was simply staying alive, keeping the Midianites from finding the food. Going through the motions of life.

I want to do more than simply stay alive.

I want to rise up out of the pit of fear and insecurity.

I want to rise up out of my guilt and shame and live standing tall.

Do you believe it yet, sweet mama? Do you believe you're loved? Do you believe you are a mighty hero? God has given you a new name, and it's all about what He is going to do in your life. Not about what you've done — good or bad. It's not about how you are going to serve Him or how you will fail Him. It's about His presence, His power and His perfection.

What name do you need to claim for yourself today?

Redeemed? God is redeeming you.

Forgiven? God has forgiven you.

Enough? God is enough for you.

Chosen? God has chosen you.

Set free? God has removed your chains. You are set free.

Holy? The blood of Jesus has made you holy and blameless as you stand before Him today.

Unafraid? Your God is with you.

Do you see how big your God is? When we truly believe that God is good and we are loved, then our *what ifs* change. We lie awake at night, restless. Not because of what we dread. But because of the possibilities of what we could do.

What if we actually made a difference in this community ...?

What if the lost were found ...?

What if our passion for Jesus won over our fear of rejection ...?

What if the blind received sight, the prisoners were set free, the broken were healed, the hopeless found hope, the lonely felt loved, the blind could see and the outcasts were invited in ...?

WHAT IF WE WERE A PART OF MAKING THIS HAPPEN?!?

What if we stopped hiding and started shining?

What if we stopped inviting that snake into our heads and instead started believing we really are who God says we are?

And what if we really believed God is who He says He is?

What if we lived standing tall, you with your feathers and me with mine, instead of trying to outperform and outshine each other?

I will protect my kids to the death. I understand my responsibility to shelter them. But for too long I've used my children as an excuse to live asleep — bound by fear, insecurity and lies.

"Who, me, God? Surely you have the wrong girl. I'm just a mama, protecting my chicks."

It's one thing to protect our children. It's another thing to hide behind them.

It's time to LIVE! **I don't want to live safe anymore. I want to live free.** But first, I must let go of my white-knuckled grip on God and the life I think I deserve.

It's taken me a long time to let go of the life I thought I would have. From the beginning, Ryan and I wanted to live a great adventure. We wanted to live outside the average American dream and do something of significance. For us, that meant living overseas. Costa Rica came quicker on the timeline than we expected, and ever since we returned home, we've been waiting for the right season to go abroad again. We are vagabonds — nomads. Looking for what's waiting just around the river bend.

The thing about rivers, though, is that there is always another bend ahead. The "dream" hasn't happened. The adventure hasn't emerged. The doors haven't opened.

But the restlessness is growing.

"God, where are You?"

In you, luv.

"I'll go wherever You want me to go, God. Just tell me!"

How about you start right where you are, luv.

Living an adventure sounds much more glamorous away from home, doesn't it?

Adventure is waiting all around us. We don't have to wait until certain things take place in our lives. We don't have to wait until we buy 40 acres in the country to live a great adventure. We don't have to move somewhere else to find it. Sometimes, adventure is waiting for us somewhere else.

But more often than not, it's waiting just at the top of the pit.

God sent Gideon to his own people. He didn't need to go far — just out of the pit.

Are you longing for something more? Are you restless to join in the song? Maybe you don't need to go far. Maybe you just need to get out of the pit.

The problem is, most of us are too scared to see it. We'd rather stay in the pit threshing wheat than climb out and set prisoners free. We're like Jacob. He wouldn't let go of his white-knuckled grip on what he thought his life should look like. He wouldn't let go until God blessed him. But once he did let go, he discovered he was already blessed. He was already lavishly loved by a good, good God. And that's when the adventure began.

Sweet one, what are you holding onto right now? What blessings are you waiting for God to give you? What circumstances in life do you believe need to fall into place before you can live out your adventure? What do you think is waiting for you just around the next bend? How are you, like Jacob, trying to control God's blessings instead of receiving what He's already given you with open hands?

In what ways are you living safe instead of living free? And when it's all said and done, do you even *want* to live free?

It's scary, I know. Our list of *what ifs* protects us, keeps us in line. Keeps us safe.

I'm sure Gideon had a whole list of *what ifs*, too.

What if the Midianites find me down here?

What if there isn't enough food and we all starve?

What if they attack again and steal everything?

What if God isn't big enough?

What if I fail?

What if they reject me?

But what if Gideon had stayed down there in that pit? What if his fear had outweighed his faith? God would still be God. And God would have rescued His people, because that's what He does.

But Gideon would still be in that pit, threshing the wheat, wondering why in Heaven's name God was not acting on his behalf.

"Where are You, God?"

In you, Gideon. Get yo' face outta the dust and go!

How has fear kept you in that pit, sweet mama? What is fear stopping you from doing? You can be a mama and change the world at the same time. Did you know that? Yes, our kids should be a priority, and yes, what you are doing inside the walls of your home matters. But I want to do more than sit on my nest. I want to do more than raise kids who grow up and sit on their nests. I want to climb up out of that pit, go in the strength I already have and set the captives free.

It starts with the three captives in my home right now.

They need to know that those chains can slip right off. But I want to teach them more than the idea of compassion. I want to show them compassion in action. I want to show them Spanx in action. The living-standing-tall, faces-to-the-sky kind of life Jesus is calling us to live.

It's happening. All around us, it's happening. Women are rising up, tired of living bent over. Tired of letting their fear determine their steps.

Mandy homeschools her three kids and raises money through an online raffle to build wells in Uganda. She's raised roughly $33,000, which will build 10 wells and provide 20 jobs for the people in Uganda. She's building her nest and changing the world at the same time.

Renae is busy with three kids in elementary school. Most days, she spends her afternoons shuttling kids from one activity to the next. She's heard Jesus' heart beating for her, though, and she's letting go of her fear. She's built relationships with her neighbors — many who don't know Jesus. They've watched her face cancer, and they know her faith isn't just words.

Why? Because they don't just see her driving to church on Sunday. They've been invited into her life, and they've seen Him through her love.

Tara's family is passionate about providing homes for children who don't have one. They've opened their home through foster care. She's given up more nights of sleep than she can count rocking babies who cry for the drugs no longer coursing through their veins. Sometimes she wonders if her kids deserve a safer life with less exposure and more attention. But her kids know what it means to be the light in a dark world. Her kids are participating in this calling. They don't just sing about how much Jesus loves the little children. They've seen it in action. And together, they're changing the world one child at a time.

Erin started a ministry to bring girls out of sex trafficking. She loves her kids, and her kids want to change the world just like their mommy. They're watching her live tall, and they want to do the same.

Anna wants to bridge the gap between the Christian community and the LGBT community. She heard her Abba's heart beating for her ... and she heard it beating for those who've been cast aside, as well. She's singing along to the tune of love, and her kids are joining the song.

Brittnie has two precious little boys, ages 2 and 1. Her days are full of chasing, cleaning and surviving. She's listening to her Abba's heart beating for her. And right now, she's changing the world one dirty diaper at a time.

None of these mamas is perfect. They all have piles of laundry, just like the rest of us. But they are listening to the heartbeat of Jesus, and they want to join His song.

All around us, women are waking up. They're telling that snake to get lost, and they're rising up — an army of mamas. Scared to death and doing it, anyway. In the strip clubs. On the streets. In churches. In schools. In communities. Their children are watching, listening and learning. And their children are catching the rhythm, too.

When you're loved by a good God, you can't help but sing along.

You were created to live standing tall, sweet mama. Get out of that pit. It's too small for you.

We are all called to different things. You might be homeschooling your children or working a 9 to 5. You might be helping in classrooms or starting ministries. You might be rocking babies in the wee hours of the morning or chasing naked toddlers down poop-smeared halls. This isn't a call to do more, be more. This is a question of how you are living the life you've been called to live.

Are you hiding behind your calling as a mom? Or are you allowing God to infuse you with His strength to fulfill His purposes for your life? Right here. Right now. *In* your calling as a mom. It won't look the same for you as it does for me. But it will look like a whole lot of mamas with straight backs rising up out of fear and marching courageously into freedom. Because God is good. And it's His untamed, outlandish, audacious, fear-squashing, snake-crushing love for us that makes us brave.

How does fear determine your steps? Is your vision for your family based on making sure nothing bad ever happens, or is it based on living life with eyes wide open and bringing God's light into a dark world? Your children are hungry to make a difference, so give them opportunities. My kids made gift bags for girls in the strip clubs. They couldn't go with me into the clubs, but they played a part. And guess what? When those girls found out that my kids loved them, too, their view of God got a whole lot bigger.

When Gideon stepped forward, believing that God could transform him into a warrior, his fear didn't disappear. He was scared to death, but kept going, anyway. That's why God gave him an army of people who would point him forward. Although Gideon's army started big, God told him to send home anyone who was too afraid.[9]

This setting captives free business is not for the faint of heart. So bring other fearless mamas along for the ride. You're going to need their support.

Gideon needed warriors surrounding him who would remind him of the truth, not tear him down. It's the same for you and me. If we want to do something brave, then we need courage spoken over us. If we want to do something that makes our knees buckle, then we need people who are going to hold us up when we can't stand up anymore. If we want to do something that makes that snake squirm, then we need some boot-stomping, scale-crushing friends who remind us just how big our God really is.

Who are you surrounded by? Do your conversations with the women in your life pull you further into the pit? Or do you walk away stronger, braver and taller? Let's not ditch our sweet friends in the pit. But if you want to stop living safe and start living free, then you might need to let some of those friends stay home. In order to live brave, you must think brave. And in order to think brave, you need women surrounding you who will remind you of your new name. Sweet one, look for friends who will draw you out of your fear instead of friends who keep you company while you wallow in your fear.

Wanna hear something else? When the army drank from the river, tired from the journey, the ones who put their faces down were sent home, too. The people who kept their faces up kept going.[10]

Those who keep their faces to the sky get to watch God move. They'll recognize when His goodness passes by.

You always have the option to stay home, mama. And by that, I don't mean our current concept of what a stay-at-home mom looks like. What I mean is, you always have the option to opt out.

God loves you. That's truer than true. He delights in you. Beyond a shadow of a doubt.

You can keep living safe. Joining the crusade doesn't give you brownie points. It doesn't get you closer to God. But get to know Him, and you'll learn His song. The longer you lean against His heartbeat, the more familiar the beat becomes. And you'll automatically start singing along.

It's a song of love. It's a song of freedom — for you and for others. And I hear it's the kind of song that gets in your head and plays on repeat. All. Day. Long.

Sweet mama, are you living safe? Or are you living free?

The time has come, mama. It's time to stand up. It's time to lift your face out of the dust and go lift the face of the mama standing next to you.

We're in a battle for hearts. And truth wins.

Every. Single. Time.

It's a scorching summer day. Steam rises from the asphalt as Gavin and I rush out of Walmart. A quick trip to the store feels like a year in an inferno in the Arizona summer.

It was supposed to be a quick trip. In and out before we continue our busy day. In the parking lot, a woman approaches us. She's holding a sign with words scrawled across it — words I've heard before. Words I've said myself too many times to count.

Help, please.

Her hair is dirty. Her cheeks are flushed with heat. I try to avoid eye contact, irritation curdling within me. We're in a hurry. Going nowhere, but trying to get there as fast as we can. But she's standing in front of our car, so I have no choice but to talk to her.

"Can you help me, please?" Her voice cracks, the words slipping through.

"What do you need?" I snap, digging for my keys in my purse.

"Some money for food. Diapers for my baby."

I shift my weight, looking around for someone else to enlist. Why did she have to stop at my car? There's a parking lot full of cars. There are people everywhere. Why me?

I want to tell her no. I want to tell her to find someone else. Does she really have a baby? How do I know what she would do with the money if I gave it to her? I look over at Gavin. His 9-year-old eyes are watching, waiting for my response.

The truth is, I don't know. I don't know her story. I don't know her pain. And then this wild, uninvited thought slashes through my suspicions, interrupting my day, my plans and my attempt to escape the heat.

Why don't you ask?

Dropping my keys back into my purse, I look into her eyes for the first time. Shielding my eyes from the sun with one hand, I beckon her close with the other.

"What happened to you?" I ask. "Why are you here, sweetie? What happened that caused you to wander through the Walmart parking lot asking for money?"

I see Hagar there in the wilderness. And I hear that same voice that called to me in the darkness. *Where have you come from, sweet one? And where are you going?*

You're not the only one who's wandered, throat parched, through the wilderness, sweet mama. You've probably passed me out there in the sand. I've probably passed you, too. We just didn't notice each other.

Startled, she looks up at me, searching my face for judgement. Searching my face for hope. I think she's searching my face for Jesus.

We lean against my car, and I listen to her story. Broken dreams. Shattered hopes. Whispers of what should have been but never was. Whispers of a life she searched for but never found. And I see myself in her eyes.

"Can I pray for you?" I ask, my arm around her sun-kissed shoulders. I lay my hand on her back, and I pray that the same God who met me in the darkness would meet her, too.

I pray, and out of the corner of my eye, I see a 9-year-old hand rise up. With eyes squeezed shut, he places his hand on her back, too.

And there we are, this boy and I. Living an adventure on a trip to Walmart.

We talk about it on the way home. He asks how we know if she really needed the money. I say, "We don't." But we know she needed Jesus. And we need never be afraid of giving Him away.

It's one thing to tell our kids about compassion. It's entirely something else when they see it in action.

It's one thing to tell our kids about truth. It's something else for them to watch us live standing tall.

It's one thing to tell our kids about Jesus. It's something else for them to smell Him on our skin.

"God, where are You?"

In you, luv. In you.

Sweet mama, the world is searching our faces for Jesus. Will it find Him there?

Digging Deeper

1. What is your list of "what ifs ..." that keeps you awake at night?

2. How has God provided a miracle for you through another person?

3. What fears are keeping you down in the pit?

4. What would happen if you stopped living safe and started living free?

5. Are you afraid of being too loved?

6. Are you waiting for something to happen before you start living an adventure now?

7. What adventure is God calling you on right where you are?

8. Can your kids smell Jesus on your skin?

Fly Back Home, Mother Hen

Sweet mama, our time is coming to an end. It's been nice, hasn't it? You and I here on the beach. I picked a good spot, didn't I? Our hair is wild from the wind. Our skin is glowing from the sun. Sink those toes in the sand one last time. Breathe deep the ocean air.

Those chicks are waiting for you. It's time to fly back home. No more drinks for you, mama. We both know you can't drink and fly at the same time. Especially considering how far we've come. But now it's time to go back home. Back home where little people need you. Back home where fights and tears and scraped-up knees need the magic only a mama can provide. You'll probably need a glass of wine later. Working magic can make a mama tired.

Look into my eyes, sweet mama. Let me hold your beautiful face in my hands. We're not the same as we were, are we? We've changed during our time together. I'm going to say it again, okay? Just in case you forget. Your Abba loves you. And He is good.

Let go of the standard you've given yourself as a mom. You don't need it anymore. Your kids don't need supermom. They just need you, a mom who's loved to death by a good God. Take the words "mom-win" and "mom-fail" out of your vocabulary. You don't need them anymore. Leave your measuring stick right there in the sand. Let the waves carry it somewhere far away.

Whatever lies you've believed about yourself, you now know where they are from. Tell that snake to take a hike. Stop inviting him into your bed. Put on your Spanx of truth, sweet one. You were made to live standing tall.

Let's meet here again soon. Let's fly the coop from time to time, sit here and bask in the sun. We need each other on this journey. I need you to lift my face out of the dust when life weighs heavy on my back.

But for now, little ones are calling. Dinner is on the stove. Activities beckon.

Sweet mama, you are doing a good job. I know most days it doesn't feel like it. But you are a good mom because you're loved by a good God. Go tell those little chicks about that good God who loves them, too.

Fly back home, mother hen. Fly back home with your face to the sky. Fly back home fearless and free. Fly back home to the adventure waiting inside your door.

Fly back home because you were made to soar.

Acknowledgments

Ryan, you've walked with me through the crazy. You've held me in the dark. You've lifted my face again and again out of the dust. You've stayed by my side when I've wanted to run. Thank you for believing in me when I didn't believe in myself. Thank you for pushing me toward my dreams when I wanted to give up. Thank you for loving me when I didn't love myself. Thank you for staying up with sick babies, picking kids up from school, bringing me tea in bed and understanding when I lost my mind. I love you. And I believe our story is only beginning.

Selah, Gavin and Emery, you've changed my world. You've taught me the song of my Abba's heart. You are loved, sweet ones. You are loved by a good God and a crazy mama. I will not show you what it means to be perfect, but I will show you what it means to be loved. Thank you for unraveling my small view of God so He could open my eyes to the mystery of grace.

Stephanie, Emilee, Brittnie and Breanna, how do I even say how much you mean to me? Thank you for showing up for 10 weeks, reading every chapter of this book and so gently telling me what needed to change. I love each of you, and those 10 weeks are tucked safely in my heart. Live standing tall, sweet girls!

Tara, you inspire me to live life to the fullest. I see Jesus in your face, and I hear His heartbeat in the way you live your life.

Justin, you have taught me what it means to wrestle with God and win. Not because we've beat Him, but because He's won over our doubt. Thank you for teaching me to question, to search and to keep believing, even when the miracles don't come.

Mom, if there ever was a supermom, it would be you. Thank you for fighting for me, showing up for me and never giving up on me. Thank you for showing me what it looks like to walk on water and to hold tight to my Abba's hand. I love you.

Dad, when you told me I could do anything, I believed you. Sometimes to your detriment, I'm sure. But I really believed that I could soar, because you told me I could. Thank you for always pushing me to be my best, for never letting me settle for less and for teaching me the value of big dreams and hard work.

Shannon, you are my heart sister. I love you, and so many of our conversations shaped this book. You are worth far more than you know.

Michelle — my boss, my editor and my friend — thank you for teaching me what true leadership looks like. You are brave, sincere, humble, kind and beautiful. I have learned so much from you over the years. Even from across the country, I can smell Jesus on your skin.

Suzanne, thank you for taking me under your wing those many years ago. When a dream was only a spark, you are the one who breathed life into a flame. Thank you for your wisdom, your friendship and your guidance. I am forever grateful.

My Jesus, oh, how I love You. Thank You for rescuing this mama trapped in the tomb of shame and insecurity. Thank You for calling me Yours and for setting me free.

Notes

Chapter 2

1. Ephesians 3:18-19, NLT
2. Sarah Bessey, *Jesus Feminist* (New York, NY: Howard Books, 2013), 114.
3. 2 Thessalonians 2:14, NLT
4. Zephaniah 3:17, NIV
5. Brennan Manning, *Abba's Child* (Colorado Springs, CO: Nav Press, 2002), 60.

Chapter 3

1. Psalm 73:1-3, MSG

Chapter 4

1. Genesis 16:1-16
2. John 6:68
3. Genesis 21:8-21
4. Genesis 21:18, NLT
5. Genesis 21:19, NLT

Chapter 5

1. John 11:1-44
2. 1 Peter 2:9
3. Stephen Smith, *The Lazarus Life* (Colorado Springs, CO: David C. Cook, 2008), 67.
4. Psalm 46:10, NLT
5. John 15:5
6. John 13:23
7. Mark 10:35-37

Chapter 6

1. Genesis 3:1
2. Matthew 3:16
3. Matthew 4:1
4. Matthew 4:1-11
5. John 8:32

Chapter 7

1. Luke 13:10-17
2. Dr. Ralph F. Wilson, *#60 Healing the Woman With a Bent Back.* Retrieved from www.jesuswalk.com.
3. Luke 13:12
4. Luke 13:13
5. Ephesians 6:10-20
6. Romans 12:12
7. Brennan Manning, *Abba's Child* (Colorado Springs, CO: Nav Press, 2002), 30.
8. Ephesians 6:13-14

Chapter 8

1. Brennan Manning, *Abba's Child* (Colorado Springs, CO: Nav Press, 2002), 148.
2. Genesis 25:26
3. Genesis 27
4. John 16:8
5. Genesis 32:26
6. Life Application Study Bible
7. Genesis 32:28, *Life Application Study Bible,* NLT.
8. Isaiah 62:1-4
9. Romans 12:2
10. Brennan Manning, *Abba's Child* (Colorado Springs, CO: Nav Press, 2002), 110.
11. Isaiah 62:3-4
12. Galatians 5:1
13. 2 Corinthians 5:17
14. Zephaniah 3:17
15. Romans 8, Revelation 12:11
16. Exodus 14:14
17. Colossians 2:12, 1 Peter 2:9-10, Colossians 1:22, Ephesians 5:27, 2 Corinthians 5:21, Ephesians 1:7, Isaiah 43:1

Chapter 9

1. I originally heard this example from Ann Voskamp's blog, *What a Mother Must Sacrifice, August 21, 2009,* www.aholyexperience.com, but you can also learn more about how mother ducks pluck their feathers at www.lakesidenaturecenter.org.
2. Genesis 33:1
3. Genesis 32:9

4. Genesis 33:10
5. Genesis 33:20
6. Sarah Bessey, *Jesus Feminist* (New York, NY: Howard Books, 2013), 127-128.

Chapter 10

1. Judges 6:13
2. Judges 6:14
3. Judges 6:15
4. Judges 6:16
5. Psalm 34:8
6. Judges 7:2-3
7. Judges 7:5-8

About the Author

Melissa studied the Bible at Capernwray Bible School in Cambridge, New Zealand. Surrounded by rolling hills, fluffy sheep, pristine beaches and unspoiled scenery, she fell in love with both Jesus and her future husband. Ryan and Melissa have now been married for 14 years. They served as missionaries in Costa Rica and now reside in Gilbert, Arizona, with their three children. There's no telling where they, now suffering from a severe case of wanderlust, will end up next.

Melissa is passionate about teaching women about their true identity in Christ. She is overly outspoken, dramatic and sensitive, and she wonders why anyone puts up with her boatload of crazy. She spent most of her life trying to be perfect and coming up short in comparison to everyone else. Now she's falling for the scandalous grace of a God who never stops pursuing her crazy, wandering, overwhelmed, learning-to-be-free heart.

Made in the USA
Lexington, KY
29 July 2016